CREATIVE CANDY MAKING

Miriam Lowenberg

WEATHERVANE BOOKS
New York

CREDIT:

Photographs on the following pages by Gordon Lowenberg/Hot Shots:
10, 25, 27, 30, 35, 37, 41, 43, 46, 51, 55, 58, 61, 66, 67, 75, 79, 83, 85, 86, 88, 95,
105, 107, 114, 120, and 125

contents

introduction

Candy-making is fun! With a few basic tools and ingredients, some spare time, and a little practice, you will be able to produce delicious, beautiful candy. There is a very deep sense of satisfaction to be had from making something from "scratch," especially confections that give such joy to your family and friends—the lucky recipients of your accomplishments.

There are some simple but important rules to follow. Read all recipes carefully—all the way through—and assemble all your ingredients and utensils before you begin. Nothing is more frustrating and wasteful than rushing into a recipe and discovering halfway through that you are out of or short of an essential ingredient. It's happened to all of us at one time or another, but the experienced cook is careful to prevent this by checking everything very carefully before starting.

Some recipes are labeled foolproof and can be made in any kind of weather; some should not be tried unless the weather is very cooperative. For making divinity, brittles, or caramels, or for dipping any kind of chocolates, try to pick a dry, clear day. If the heat is on in the house, turn the thermostat down to 65. Air conditioning makes summer candy-making more realistic than it was before cooled homes were so common, but do not have the kitchen too cool. Again, 65 is about right. Remember that heat and moisture are the enemies of candy-making.

Before combining ingredients, lightly oil the saucepan you are going to use. I find the easiest way to do this is to spray the pan with one of the new no-stick sprays. I use these on everything from saucepans to knives and spatulas. Oiling the saucepan helps to keep sugar crystals from forming above the liquid line and also helps to keep the mixture from burning or boiling over.

Mix together all the specified ingredients in the proper pan before heating; then, unless otherwise specified, stir constantly while the sugar is melting and the mixture comes to a boil. Stirring will keep the sugar from burning before it is completely dissolved, and it will allow the mixture to heat through evenly. Where syrup has splashed above the liquid line, sugar crystals will form, and it is very important to wash these down carefully before the mixture is allowed to boil to the final stage. I find the best way to do this is to dip a clean pastry brush into cold water and gently brush off the accumulated crystals.

Do not cover candy mixtures while cooking unless so directed. The reason for covering sugar-and-water syrup for a minute or two at a specific point in the recipe is to allow steam that forms under the lid to wash down accumulated sugar crystals. Do this only when directed.

Stirring is best done with a long-handled wooden spoon. You will be dealing with a very hot mixture, and a metal spoon would soon become too hot to hold. Also, a wooden spoon is very kind to the saucepan—it will not scratch. A long handle will help keep your hand away from the heat.

A candy thermometer is really almost essential, although with experience you can learn to use the cold-water method to determine the stage the syrup has reached. I always use a thermometer. Mine has a clip that slides so that it can be used on any size saucepan. It is marked in both F and C degrees and in stages; i.e., soft ball and hard ball. This is a very accurate measure that takes all guesswork out of candy-making, and I think it is well worth the small investment. Almost all hardware stores and houseware departments sell candy thermometers in several sizes. I would recommend one with a clip and a protected mercury ball so that it doesn't break easily. When using a candy thermometer always read it "head on," never on the slant, to get an accurate reading.

Remove the pan from the heat as soon as the proper temperature is reached, and follow the rest of the directions in the recipe. Never scrape the mixture from the pan, as this causes sugar crystals to form and tends to make grainy instead of smooth and creamy candy.

Add flavorings, unless otherwise directed, during the final process, after the mixture has cooled a little. Most flavorings are very volatile, and, if added to hot mixtures, much of the flavor goes up in steam.

Colors are generally added to fondants, jellies, and marzipan during the mixing or kneading stage. Liquid colors can be painted onto the surface of finished, shaped marzipan with a very fine, clean artist's brush.

I hope you have an admiring audience to lick the pans and spoons. I treasure the memory of my four-year-old granddaughter, chocolaty face beaming up at me, saying "Grandmama, it's so much fun visiting you!" More than enough reward for the effort put into homemade candy.

assorted candies

utensils

saucepans

I hope you already have several saucepans with heavy bottoms for even heat distribution; this type is especially important for candy-making. The most-used sizes are a 1½- to 2-quart and a 3-quart pan; for making brittles, I use a 5-quart Dutch oven. Most veteran homemakers already have these standard-size pans; if you don't, give serious consideration to buying one or two basic saucepans of very good quality. They will be valuable for all cooking, not just for candy-making. I have one stainless-steel, copper-clad saucepan that is 30 years old. I have used it daily for all that time and have polished the bottom so many times that the trademark has long since disappeared. It was expensive to start with, but in the long run it is probably the most economical purchase I ever made!

double boiler

A double boiler is useful for melting chocolate. If you do not have one, you can improvise by using a heat-resistant bowl that fits over a small saucepan, but remember that it is possible for steam to get into the chocolate this way, and just one drop of moisture is enough to cause streaking in the chocolate when it cools. Streaking does not affect the taste, but it doesn't look very nice, so for melting and tempering chocolate for dipping, I prefer to use a double boiler that is fitted securely so that no steam escapes from the bottom.

shallow pan

You will need a shallow pan or two to cool fudge and caramels and to mold marshmallows and jellies. The most useful sizes are 8 × 8 × 2 inches and 11¾ × 7½ × 1¾ inches. These are standard sizes for glass heat-resistant pans, but any similar size will do. A 9 × 12-inch *jelly-roll pan* is also very useful.

measuring spoons and cups

Accurate measuring is very important in candy-making, so a good set of measuring spoons and cups is a must. No matter how accurate the cups are, each one is slightly different, so I always use the same cup to measure all ingredients in a recipe. I start with dry and end with liquid so that I don't have to stop and wash the cup while I'm working.

wooden spoons

Stirring should be done with a wooden spoon. I have a large collection of various sizes—old friends that I wouldn't be without.

sharp knives, scissors, and a cutting board

Sharp knives, scissors, and a cutting board have their obvious uses.

spatulas

Ordinary spatulas have a limited use in candy-making. You will need a heavy spatula for processing fondants and some brittles; for this most candy-makers buy a sturdy *paint scraper* with a 3- to 5-inch blade.

dipping fork

For dipping chocolates you can buy a special dipping fork; however, many really fine chocolates are hand-dipped, and I do mean fingers! I use both a fork and my fingers and try very hard not to lick until I'm all done!

food-processor

If you are the lucky owner of a food-processor, by all means use it—for grating, slicing, and chopping, following the instructions that came with it. If you don't have a processor, a good *hand grater* is a valuable addition to your kitchen.

electric mixer

I am fortunate in having a heavy-duty electric mixer that is equipped with a balloon beater, a paddle beater, and a bread hook. Since I am essentially lazy, I use the paddle for beating candy and the bread hook for kneading. Of course the balloon beater is essential for making marshmallows and beating egg whites for kisses. Lacking an electric mixer, you will have to depend on hand beating and kneading, which is fine for everything but marshmallows or divinity, two candies I would not attempt without an electric mixer.

marble slab, cookie tin, and cooling rack

If you have a marble slab to use in dipping chocolates or for pouring hot fondants and brittles onto, congratulations! You own an almost perfect surface for candy-making. If you do not have a marble slab, and most homemakers do not, you can use a large cookie tin placed on a cooling rack. This allows air to circulate and cool the mixture evenly and also protects the surface under the pan from burning.

candy thermometer

Last but not least you should have a reliable, easy-to-use candy thermometer. With all the guesswork taken out of temperature-measuring, you can relax and be sure your time and ingredients will not be wasted.

some utensils and ingredients

ingredients

granulated sugar

Any granulated sugar can be used in candy-making. It's usually wise to sift it before measuring, so that lumps can be broken up. However, if the sugar you are using seems very fine and lump-free, you can measure it directly from the canister or container. I always bury a slit vanilla bean in my canister of sugar. It gives a very delicate and subtle flavor and aroma to the sugar but does not replace the vanilla flavoring called for in many recipes.

light and dark brown sugar

Light and dark brown sugar are the same except for degree of flavor, but I almost always use light brown sugar for candy-making, as the flavor is milder. It should be moist and easily handled and packed down very firmly into the measuring cup for accurate measuring. Today most brown sugar is packaged in plastic to help prevent caking and lumping, but, if you happen to have a box of brown sugar that has solidified, try an old housewife's remedy. Put a large slice of fresh apple into the bag with the sugar. Seal it tightly and let it stand for about a day. This will usually soften the sugar to a usable state.

confectioners' sugar

Confectioners' sugar is extremely fine sugar with cornstarch added. Use it only where specifically called for—*never* substitute confectioners' sugar for granulated or brown sugar. Always sift it before measuring.

corn syrup

Corn syrup is used in many candy recipes to help prevent graininess. Do not substitute dark corn syrup for light.

honey

When honey is called for in a recipe, any liquid honey can be used, but remember that the flavor of the honey will affect the flavor of the candy. Do not use creamed honey or honey spreads.

molasses

Any kind of molasses can be used in a recipe where molasses is specified.

milk

Where milk is called for, I have used fresh skimmed milk plus at least 2 tablespoons of margarine for each cup of milk. The margarine replaces the butter fat that is present in whole milk. This is already taken into account in each recipe. You can also use dried, reconstituted skimmed milk. Whole milk or light cream can be used in the same amount for a richer candy. Canned evaporated milk can be substituted for whole milk but should be diluted half-and-half with water. In some recipes evaporated milk is specified; in these recipes it should be used just as is, from the can.

margarine

I have used unsalted non-dairy margarine in every recipe calling for margarine. You can substitute salted margarine or *butter*; however, if you use a salted product, omit the salt from the recipe. Do not use whipped or diet products, as the volume is completely different.

chocolate

Chocolate comes in a great variety—sweet, semisweet, and unsweetened 1-ounce squares; milk or semisweet chocolate bits; cocoa; and candy bars. Any reliable brand of chocolate can be used, but be sure to use the type specified in the recipe. Chocolate bits can not be substituted for squares, and it is always best to use the kind of chocolate that is called for; i.e., sweet, semisweet, or unsweetened. You can substitute cocoa by using ¼ cup cocoa plus ½ teaspoon shortening for each ounce of chocolate. If you are going to be making a lot of candy or dipping a large quantity, it is possible to buy dipping chocolate in 10-pound bars from a candy-supplier. This is also available in several different kinds of chocolate. If you are interested in buying in this quantity, consult the Yellow Pages of your telephone directory under Candy and Confectionery—Wholesale to find a supplier in your area.

baking soda

Baking soda is used in some candy recipes to produce a lovely honeycomb texture—usually in brittles. Be sure to use a large enough saucepan for this type of candy; the mixture foams as the baking soda is added. Since moisture from steam can cause baking soda to cake and stick to a measuring spoon, I give the spoon a good whack on the edge of the pan as I add the soda and then look at the spoon to be sure all the soda is gone.

raisins, dried fruits, candied peels and fruits

Raisins, dried fruits, candied peels and fruits can all be used in many varieties of candy. A good source for most fruit in bulk quantities is a health-food store. To cut or slice dried or candied fruit easily, I use sharp scissors that I occasionally dip into hot water.

nuts

Nuts are a very important addition to many candies, adding and changing taste and texture. Be sure the nuts you use are fresh; rancid or stale nuts can spoil an otherwise delicious batch of candy. I'm very lazy about shelling nuts, since I use large quantities, so I usually buy shelled, unsalted nuts in bulk at my favorite health-food store. I always roast them, very lightly, as I use them. I've found that the simplest thing to do is to spread the quantity of nuts I need on a lightly oiled cookie tin, put them into the oven, heat to 300°F, turn off the oven, and leave the nuts in for about 10 or 15 minutes. I chop nuts in a food processor, watching very carefully so they won't be ground instead of chopped. I grate nuts with a Mouli grater. I never use a grinder or blender, although some cooks do, because I do not like the thick rather oily paste that results from this process. If you have a very good wrist and a sharp chef's knife, you can chop nuts on a cutting board. For most fudge it is not necessary to chop the nuts ahead of time, because when you cut the cooled fudge into pieces you will slice right through the nuts.

flavorings

Only your imagination will limit your use of flavorings. *Vanilla* is the standby and is used either alone or to enhance other flavors, but look around you at home and in the grocery store; you will find dozens of other ideas. Any kind of *whiskey* or *liqueur* can be used—*peppermint patties* are great, but how about *creme de menthe patties* for the grown-ups? *Instant coffee powder* is one of my favorites and turns chocolate into mocha. I like to combine grated rinds with the same flavor extract for an underlined taste. Remember one important rule—add the flavor to a cooled syrup if at all possible, so you don't lose most of it in steam. If the recipe calls for the flavoring to be added to the hot mixture, it will specify a larger amount to compensate for the loss.

colors

Vegetable colors come in three forms: dry, paste, and liquid. You will be most familiar with the liquid drops that can be bought in almost all grocery stores. The four primary colors are packaged together, and you will have to mix them to make other colors and shades. The result is usually pastel rather than strong. *Paste colors* can be bought in many gourmet shops specializing in special bakeware. Again, you can mix the primary colors to get any color you want, and with paste colors it is possible to get a stronger shade. I never use *powder colors* and do not recommend them. The following is a very simple *color chart* to get you started, but by all means experiment on your own for many shades.

> Orange = 1 part red + 3 parts yellow
> Purple = 3 parts red + 1 part blue
> Brown = 3 parts red + 2 parts yellow + 2 parts green

temperature chart

Even though a candy thermometer is essential for accurate temperature-testing, it is very valuable to learn to test for "doneness" by the cold-water method so you will be able to determine proper cooking stages by feel.

Using a dish of cold, not ice, water, test by dropping a little boiling syrup into the water and forming it into a ball with your fingers. At the *soft-ball* stage you will be able to pick up the ball, but it will fall apart as soon as you take it out of the water. At the *firm-ball* stage the ball will be pliable in the water and will hold its shape out of the water. At the *hard-ball* stage the ball will be quite hard, and, when you take it out of the water, you will be able to tap it against the side of the dish without it's breaking. At the *soft-crack* stage the candy is too hard to form into a ball in the water and will "ribbon" when you lift it out. At the *hard-crack* stage it will be brittle when you take it out of the water. At the *caramel* stage the syrup begins to turn to an amber color, darkening very quickly. You must watch it very carefully at this stage so that it does not burn.

While you are testing in cold water, take the syrup off the heat; it can go from stage to stage rapidly, which can result in overcooking.

Soft-ball stage	234 – 238°F
Firm-ball stage	245 – 250°F
Hard-ball stage	250 – 265°F
Soft-crack stage	265 – 272°F
Hard-crack stage	290 – 310°F
Caramel	315 – 345°F

If you live at an altitude above 2,000 feet, you must make the appropriate adjustment in temperature to obtain the best results in candy-making. Since this changes for each 1,000 feet in altitude, it will be necessary for you to check with your local experts to obtain the proper adjustment. The home-economic department of any school or university should be able to give you the exact information.

fudge

Fudge! The very word brings back memories of childhood, the excitement of watching your mother, grandmother, or big sister work magic with chocolate, sugar, and milk, turning simple ingredients into fragrant, delicious candy. What can match the memory of first the smell and then the taste of creamy fudge? Today people are anxious to recapture some of the charm and delight of an earlier time, taking pride in the do-it-yourself craftsmanship of "homemades," whether it be clothes, bread, or candy. Homemade fudge is a wonderful place to start. With a few simple utensils and ingredients, easy-to-follow recipes, and a little time, it is possible to turn out candy that will receive an enthusiastic reception from your lucky family and friends.

The general directions for candy-making should be followed—read the recipe carefully and organize all equipment and ingredients you are going to use before you start. It is important to time the boiling period carefully in the "foolproof" recipes and to watch the temperature carefully in the temperature-controlled recipes. During the boiling and cooling periods, it is very important not to stir or shake the mixture any more than absolutely necessary, because this is when sugar crystals form. Fudge should be creamy, not grainy, and the formation of crystals produces the grainy texture. After the mixture has cooled to lukewarm, that is, 110°F, the beating process starts; this is where the magic takes place. You will start with a fairly thin, glossy syrup, and, as you beat, the mixture will thicken and lose its glossy look. This is your goal! At this point it should be spread in a well-oiled pan and allowed to cool completely and harden. Warm, thick fudge can also be kneaded for extra creaminess. Kneaded fudge can be rolled into logs or formed into other shapes. Fudge balls are used for dipping or for rolling in ground nuts, cocoa, or anything that takes your fancy. After the fudge has cooled completely in the pan, it can be cut into traditional fudge-shaped squares—or into other shapes that you may like.

Once in a while even the most experienced candy-maker finds that the fudge has not hardened properly in the pan. If this happens to you, do not worry—there are one or two remedies. If the fudge is still warm, but you are afraid it will never harden properly, you can scrape it out of the pan onto a cookie tin and knead it, just as you would knead bread, until it is firm. If it seems too sticky to knead by hand, or if it has cooled completely and is still not firm enough to cut into squares, I take dramatic action. I scrape the mixture into an oiled saucepan and heat it very slowly, stirring to keep it from sticking or overheating on the bottom while the top stays cool. When the mixture is melted and still just warm, I remove it from the heat and beat in ¾ cup of marshmallows, either standard or mini size. I continue beating until the mixture is very thick. If the marshmallows do not completely melt, it's all right. The little flecks of marshmallow that remain make a very interesting and good fudge.

All fudge keeps very well if it is stored in an airtight container in a cool place. As a matter of fact fudge should be aged for a day or two before serving, as the flavor improves during this time. Before birthdays or holidays I make several varieties ahead of time and store them, each kind in a separate container. My only problem—and it will be yours, too—is to keep my "customers" from invading the storage closet!

Fudge generally travels well, although I don't think I would try to mail any candy during hot summer months. When I want to send fudge as a sweet treat, I use an aluminum-foil pan—the nice kind that you can buy with a plastic lid that fits very tightly—to spread the fudge in to cool. I do not slice it into squares, but leave that to be done when the fudge arrives.

fudge

traditional chocolate fudge

Yield: 1¼ pounds

2 1-ounce squares unsweetened chocolate
2 cups sugar
1 cup milk
1 tablespoon light corn syrup
Dash of salt
2 tablespoons margarine
1 teaspoon vanilla
Dash of nutmeg (optional)

Lightly oil inside of 1½- to 2-quart saucepan. Combine chocolate, sugar, milk, corn syrup, and salt in saucepan. Cook over medium heat, stirring constantly, until sugar dissolves and mixture comes to boil. Wash down crystals on inside of pan above liquid line, using clean pastry brush dipped in water. If using candy thermometer, clip it onto pan and allow mixture to cook until thermometer registers 238°F (soft-ball stage). If not using candy thermometer, test for soft-ball stage (syrup forms soft ball in cold water). Do not stir while mixture is cooking; when it reaches proper temperature, remove from heat immediately. Add margarine, *but do not stir.* Cool to 110°F. If not using thermometer, cool until bottom of pan feels lukewarm. Add vanilla and nutmeg. Start beating vigorously; beat until mixture loses its glossy look. Pour into well-oiled 8 × 8 × 2-inch pan. Cut into squares when cool.

I have been very successful with beating this fudge in my electric mixer. As it becomes very thick, I change the beater to a bread hook and knead the fudge just like bread dough until it is very creamy and can be shaped by hand. Your imagination can take over then. Sometimes I make small fudge balls and roll them in cocoa or chopped nuts. A nice change from traditional fudge squares is a fudge roll: form long sausage-shaped roll and slice into rounds. Roll can be coated with chopped nuts or shredded coconut, then sliced.

Store in airtight container in cool place. Try to keep tasters away from it for a day or two to allow flavor to develop.

chocolate-nut fudge

Mix 1 cup of your favorite unsalted, roasted nuts into fudge after it is beaten and before it is spread in the pan to cool. If you use the kneaded method, nuts can be kneaded into fudge.

mocha fudge

Add 1 teaspoon instant coffee to mixture as it cooks.

foolproof chocolate fudge*

Yield: 1¼ pounds

1⅔ cups sugar
⅔ cup evaporated milk
1 6-ounce package semisweet
    chocolate bits
1½ cups miniature marshmallows
Dash of salt
Dash of nutmeg
4 tablespoons margarine

Lightly oil inside of 1½- to 2-quart saucepan. Combine sugar and milk in saucepan; cook over medium heat, stirring constantly, until sugar is completely dissolved and mixture comes to boil. Boil, stirring constantly, 5 minutes. Remove from heat; add chocolate bits, marshmallows, salt, nutmeg, and margarine. Stir until chocolate and marshmallows are melted. Beat until thick and not glossy. Spread in oiled 8 × 8 × 2-inch pan. When cool, cut into squares.

This fudge can be cooled in the refrigerator and should be stored in the refrigerator in very hot weather. Bring it to room temperature before serving.

foolproof chocolate-coconut fudge

After fudge has been cut into squares, roll each square in shredded coconut.

foolproof chocolate-fruit fudge

Mix 1 cup raisins, chopped candied fruit, dates, figs, or any kind of dried fruit into fudge before spreading mixture into pan.

foolproof chocolate-marshmallow fudge

Spread 1 cup miniature marshmallows on bottom of well-oiled pan before spreading fudge mixture in pan.

foolproof chocolate-nut fudge

Mix 1 cup of your favorite nuts into fudge mixture before spreading.

*This recipe will work no matter what the weather.

cocoa-honey fudge

Yield: 1½ pounds

⅔ cup cocoa
3 cups sugar
1½ cups milk
½ cup honey
Dash of salt
2 tablespoons margarine
1 teaspoon vanilla

Lightly oil inside of 2- to 3-quart saucepan. Combine cocoa, sugar, milk, honey, and salt in saucepan. Cook over medium heat, stirring constantly, until sugar is completely dissolved and all ingredients well blended. Let mixture come to boil, stirring periodically to keep mixture blended. When syrup comes to boil, wipe down sugar crystals above liquid line, using clean pastry brush dipped in cold water. Clip on candy thermometer; cook until soft-ball stage (238°F) is reached. Remove from heat immediately. Add margarine, *but do not stir.* Let cool to 110°F or until bottom of pan is just warm to touch. Add vanilla; beat vigorously until mixture is thick and loses glossy look. Pour into well-oiled pan about 12 × 8 × 2 inches. Cut into squares when cool.

cocoa-honey coconut fudge

Add ½ cup shredded coconut to fudge mixture before it is poured into pan.

cocoa-honey fruit fudge

Add ½ cup raisins or ½ cup chopped or diced candied fruit to fudge mixture before it is spread to cool. Candied orange peel is especially good with this fudge, and for a really different taste try chopped candied gingerroot.

cocoa-honey marshmallow fudge

Spread 1½ cups miniature marshmallows on bottom of pan before spreading fudge to cool.

cocoa-honey nut fudge

Add 1 cup broken nut meats to mixture just before spreading to cool.

chocolate non-dairy fudge

This is a no-nonsense name for a very unique fudge that contains no animal fat if non-dairy margarine is used. It is a very creamy fudge with a very fine flavor.

Yield: 1¼ pounds

2 1-ounce squares unsweetened
    chocolate
2 cups sugar
1 cup non-dairy creamer
1 tablespoon light corn syrup

Dash of salt
2 tablespoons margarine
1 teaspoon vanilla
1 cup firmly packed marshmallows,
    miniature or standard

Lightly oil inside of 1½- to 2-quart saucepan. Combine chocolate, sugar, non-dairy creamer, corn syrup, and salt in saucepan. Cook over medium heat, stirring constantly, until sugar dissolves and mixture comes to boil. Wash down sugar crystals above liquid line, using clean pastry brush dipped in cold water. Clip on candy thermometer; cook, without stirring, until thermometer registers 238°F (soft-ball stage). If not using thermometer, test for soft-ball stage using cold-water test. (See Temperature Chart.) Remove from heat at once. Add margarine, *but do not stir.* Cool to 110°F or until bottom of pan feels warm to touch. Add vanilla and marshmallows; beat vigorously until mixture thickens and loses its glossy look. It's okay if marshmallows do not completely dissolve. Bits of marshmallow in fudge make an interesting texture and taste. Spread thickened mixture into well-oiled 8 × 8 × 2-inch pan; cut into squares when cool. Store in airtight container in a cool place.

non-dairy chocolate-nut fudge

Add 1 cup broken unsalted, roasted nuts to mixture as you beat it.

non-dairy mocha fudge

Add 1 teaspoon instant coffee to mixture as it cooks.

foolproof butterscotch fudge*

Yield: 1¼ pounds

1⅔ cups firmly packed light
    brown sugar
⅔ cup evaporated milk
1 6-ounce package butterscotch bits

½ cups miniature marshmallows
4 tablespoons margarine
Dash of salt
1 teaspoon vanilla

Lightly oil inside of 1½- to 2-quart saucepan. Combine sugar and milk in saucepan; cook over medium heat, stirring constantly, until sugar is completely dissolved
20

and mixture comes to boil. Boil, stirring constantly, 5 minutes. At this point mixture may look curdled, but *do not worry;* as you beat, it will become creamy. Remove from heat. Add butterscotch bits, marshmallows, margarine, and salt. Stir until butterscotch bits and marshmallows are melted. Add vanilla. Beat until thick, cool, and not glossy. Pour into well-oiled 8 × 8 × 2-inch pan. Cut into squares when cool.

This fudge can be cooled in refrigerator; also can be stored in refrigerator during very hot weather. Allow it to come to room temperature before serving.

foolproof butterscotch caramel-nut fudge

Mix 1 cup of your favorite unsalted, roasted nuts into fudge mixture before spreading in pan to cool. Walnuts are particularly good with caramel fudge.

Instead of mixing nuts through fudge, place ½ walnut on top of each piece of fudge.

foolproof butterscotch marshmallow-caramel fudge

Spread 1 cup miniature marshmallows on bottom of oiled pan before spreading fudge in pan.

*This recipe will work no matter what the weather.

foolproof wicked delight

This confection is very rich and devilishly good! It keeps very well stored in an airtight container in a cool place.

Yield: 2 pounds

    2 4-ounce bars Baker's German sweet
        chocolate
    1 cup miniature marshmallows
    1 cup roasted unsalted almonds
    1 recipe Foolproof Chocolate Fudge
        (see Index)

Melt chocolate bars in top of double boiler over hot, not boiling, water. Stir to blend; pour half of chocolate into well-oiled 8 × 8 × 2-inch pan. Keep remainder of melted chocolate warm. The easiest way to do this is to leave unused chocolate in top of double boiler and place it over warm water. Allow chocolate in pan to cool and set. Arrange nuts and marshmallows over cooled chocolate.

Prepare fudge as directed; pour over nuts and chocolate. Cool in refrigerator about 15 minutes. Pour remaining melted chocolate over fudge layer. As it cools, you can score top for cutting. Cool thoroughly; cut into squares.

maple fudge

This is a favorite of my New England daughter!

Yield: 1 pound

> **2 cups sugar**
> **½ cup pure maple syrup**
> **(maple-flavored sugar syrup will not do)**
> **1 cup milk**
> **2 tablespoons light corn syrup**
> **Dash of salt**
> **2 tablespoons margarine**
> **1 teaspoon vanilla**

Lightly oil inside of 1½- to 2-quart saucepan. Combine sugar, maple syrup, milk, corn syrup, and salt in pan. Cook over low heat until sugar is completely dissolved and mixture comes to boil. Wipe down sugar crystals above liquid line, using clean pastry brush dipped in cold water. Clip on candy thermometer; cook, without stirring, until soft-ball stage (238°F). Remove from heat immediately. Add margarine, *but do not stir.* Cool to 110°F or until bottom of pan feels just warm to touch. Add vanilla; beat vigorously until thick and mixture has lost glossy look. Spread in well-oiled 8 × 8 × 2-inch pan to cool. Cut into squares when cool.

maple-nut fudge

This fudge is particularly good with walnuts. Add 1 cup broken walnut meats to fudge just before spreading to cool.

yogurt fudge

Here is another use for a current favorite.

Yield: 1 pound

> **2 cups firmly packed light brown**
> **sugar**
> **1 cup unflavored yogurt**
> **Dash of salt**
> **2 tablespoons margarine**
> **1 cup firmly packed marshmallows,**
> **miniature or standard**
> **1 teaspoon vanilla**

Lightly oil inside of 1½- to 2-quart saucepan. Combine sugar, yogurt, and salt in pan. Cook over low heat, stirring constantly, until sugar is completely dissolved and mixture comes to boil. Wipe down sugar crystals above liquid line, using clean pastry brush dipped in cold water. Cook until mixture reaches soft-ball stage (238°F). If syrup looks curdled, *do not worry*; it will become creamy as it is beaten. Remove from heat immediately. Add margarine and marshmallows; *do not stir.*

Allow mixture to cool to 110°F or until pan feels warm to touch. Add vanilla; beat vigorously until fudge is thick and has lost glossy look. Pour into 8 × 8 × 2-inch pan to cool. Cut into squares when cool.

yogurt-nut fudge

Add ½ cup chopped or broken nut meats to mixture before spreading in pan to cool.

foolproof peanut fudge*

Yield: 1¼ pounds

1⅔ cups firmly packed light brown
    sugar
⅔ cup evaporated milk
1 6-ounce package peanut chips
1½ cups miniature marshmallows
4 tablespoons margarine
Dash of salt
1 teaspoon vanilla

Lightly oil inside of 1½- to 2-quart saucepan. Combine sugar and milk in saucepan; cook over medium heat, stirring constantly, until sugar is completely dissolved and mixture comes to full boil. Boil, stirring constantly, 5 minutes. If mixture looks curdled, *do not worry*; as you beat, mixture will become creamy. Remove from heat. Add peanut chips, marshmallows, margarine, and salt; stir until peanut chips and marshmallows are melted. Add vanilla; beat until thick and cool and mixture loses glossy look. Pour into well-oiled 8 × 8 × 2-inch pan. When cool, cut into squares.

This fudge can be cooled in refrigerator, and in very hot weather can be stored in refrigerator. Be sure to bring it to room temperature before serving.

foolproof peanut chocolate-freak fudge

For those who think candy isn't candy unless it's chocolate, substitute ½ cup milk-chocolate bits for ½ cup marshmallows. This doesn't hide the peanut flavor but adds a special touch.

foolproof peanut-freak fudge

For peanut freaks, stir 1 cup unsalted, roasted peanuts into fudge before spreading it in pan to cool.

---

*This recipe will work no matter what the weather.

sour-cream fudge

This very creamy fudge has a most distinctive flavor and is not too sweet.

Yield: 1 pound

2 cups sugar	2 tablespoons margarine
Dash of salt	1 teaspoon vanilla
¾ cup commercial sour cream	

Lightly oil inside of 1½- to 2-quart saucepan. Combine sugar, salt, and sour cream in pan. Cook over low heat, stirring constantly, until sugar is completely dissolved and mixture comes to boil. Wipe down sugar crystals above liquid line, using clean pastry brush dipped in cold water. Clip on candy thermometer; cook to soft-ball stage (238°F). Remove from heat immediately. Add margarine, *but do not stir.* Cool to 110°F or until pan feels just warm to touch. Add vanilla; beat vigorously until mixture is thick and has lost glossy look. Spread in well-oiled 8 × 8 × 2-inch pan; cut into squares when cool.

sour-cream chocolate-chip fudge

Add ½ cup semisweet chocolate chips (miniature chips are perfect) to fudge before spreading to cool.

sour-cream nut fudge

Add ½ cup chopped or broken nut meats to fudge before spreading in pan to cool.

milk-chocolate sour-cream fudge

Try this for a completely different taste.

Yield: 1¼ pounds

2 cups sugar	2 tablespoons margarine
1 cup commercial sour cream	¾ cup milk-chocolate bits
Dash of salt	1 teaspoon vanilla

Lightly oil inside of 1½- to 2-quart saucepan. Combine sugar, sour cream, and salt in pan. Cook over low heat, stirring constantly, until sugar is dissolved and mixture has come to boil. Wipe down sugar crystals above liquid line, using clean pastry brush dipped in cold water. Clip on candy thermometer; cook to soft-ball stage (238°F). Remove from heat. Add margarine and chocolate bits; *do not stir.* Cool to 110°F or until bottom of pan is cool to touch. Add vanilla; beat vigorously until mixture is thick and has lost glossy look. Spread in well-oiled 8 × 8 × 2-inch pan to cool. Cut into squares when cool.

rum-raisin milk-chocolate sour-cream fudge

Substitute 1 tablespoon rum or 1 teaspoon rum flavoring for vanilla. Add ½ cup raisins to mixture before spreading it to cool.

light fudge

light fudge

Yield: 1 pound

> **2 cups sugar**
> **⅔ cup milk**
> **2 tablespoons light corn syrup**
> **Dash of salt**
> **2 tablespoons margarine**
> **1 teaspoon vanilla**

Lightly oil inside of 1½- to 2-quart saucepan. Combine sugar, milk, corn syrup, and salt in pan. Cook over low heat, stirring constantly, until sugar is completely dissolved and mixture comes to boil. Wipe down sugar crystals above liquid line, using clean pastry brush dipped in cold water. Clip on candy thermometer; cook to 238°F (soft-ball stage). Remove from heat immediately. Add margarine, *but do not stir*. Cool to 110°F or until bottom of pan is just warm to touch. Add vanilla; beat vigorously until syrup becomes thick and loses its glossy look. Spread into well-oiled 8 × 8 × 2-inch pan; cut into squares when cool. This fudge can also be kneaded at this stage, then formed into fudge balls or rolled and sliced.

variations

Because this fudge is essentially plain, it is a very fine base for adding a variety of flavors and/or textures. You can substitute any flavor for the vanilla and add anything your imagination dictates. Cut into squares when cool. Decorated with half of a walnut or pecan, this fudge makes a simple but elegant addition to any sweet tray.

penuche

One of the classic candies.

Yield: 1 pound

2 cups firmly packed light brown sugar
¾ cup milk
1 tablespoon light corn syrup
Dash of salt
2 tablespoons margarine
1 teaspoon vanilla
1 cup broken nut meats

Lightly oil inside of 2-quart saucepan. Combine sugar, milk, corn syrup, and salt in pan. Cook over medium heat, stirring constantly, until sugar is completely dissolved and mixture comes to boil. Wash down sugar crystals above liquid line, using clean pastry brush dipped in cold water. Clip on candy thermometer; cook mixture to soft-ball stage (238°F). If syrup looks curdled, *do not worry*; it will become creamy as it is beaten. Remove from heat immediately. Add margarine; *do not stir*. Cool to 110°F or until pan feels warm to touch. Add vanilla; beat vigorously until mixture becomes thick and loses glossy look. Add nuts; spread in well-oiled 8 × 8 × 2-inch pan to cool. Cut into squares when cool.

Almost fudge, but not quite. Some candy-lovers think it is even better! What else but—pralines! Nibbling on one sparks instant recall of New Orleans. Sip a cup of hot, black, chicory-flavored coffee as an accompaniment and you have a perfect ending for any meal.

pralines

basic pralines

Yield: 12 large or 24 small pralines

2 cups firmly packed light
brown sugar
¾ cup light cream or ¾ cup
undiluted evaporated milk

1 tablespoon margarine
1 cup pecans

Lightly oil inside of 2-quart saucepan. Combine sugar and cream in pan. Cook over low heat, stirring constantly, until sugar is completely dissolved. Wipe down sugar crystals above the liquid line, using clean pastry brush dipped in cold water. Clip on candy thermometer; cook without stirring until thermometer registers 236°F (soft-ball stage). Remove from heat. Add margarine and pecans; beat with wooden spoon just until mixture begins to thicken and "whiten." It is important not to over-beat, because mixture will become too thick to drop by spoonful. Using tablespoon for very large pralines or teaspoon for smaller ones, drop by spoonful onto well-greased cookie tin; cool until firm. Store in airtight container in cool place.

coffee pralines

Add 1 teaspoon instant coffee crystals to sugar; proceed with recipe.

crisp pralines

Substitute water for cream for more-brittle texture.

light pralines

Substitute granulated sugar for brown sugar. Add 1 teaspoon vanilla with margarine.

walnut pralines

Substitute 1 cup walnuts for pecans.

maple pralines

Yield: 24 small pralines

2 cups confectioners' sugar
1 cup pure maple syrup
¾ cup light cream or ¾ cup undiluted evaporated milk
1 tablespoon margarine
1½ cups pecans

Lightly oil inside of 2-quart saucepan. Combine sugar, syrup, and cream in pan. Cook over low heat, stirring constantly, until sugar is dissolved and mixture comes to boil. Wipe down sugar crystals above liquid line, using clean pastry brush dipped in cold water. Clip on candy thermometer; cook mixture, without stirring, until thermometer registers 236°F (soft-ball stage). Remove from heat. Add margarine and pecans; beat with wooden spoon just until mixture thickens a little and begins to look cloudy. Drop by teaspoon onto well-oiled cookie tin; cool until firm. Store in airtight container in cool place.

maple-brandy pralines

Add 2 tablespoons brandy to mixture as you beat.

maple-rum pralines

Add 2 tablespoons rum to mixture as you beat.

maple-sherry pralines

Add 1 tablespoon sherry wine to mixture as you beat.

maple-walnut pralines

Substitute walnuts for pecans.

yogurt pralines

Yield: 12 to 15 pralines

3 cups sugar	2 tablespoons margarine
½ teaspoon baking soda	1 teaspoon vanilla
1 cup unflavored yogurt	2 cups pecans
2 tablespoons light corn syrup	

Lightly oil inside of 4-quart saucepan. (This is going to foam!) Combine sugar, soda, yogurt, and corn syrup in pan. Cook over low heat, stirring constantly, until sugar is dissolved. Wipe off sugar crystals above liquid line, using clean pastry brush dipped in cold water. Allow mixture to come to boil. Clip on candy thermometer; cook until thermometer registers 234°F (soft-ball stage). Remove from heat. Stir in margarine, vanilla, and pecans. Beat with wooden spoon just until mixture thickens and begins to look cloudy. Drop by spoonful onto well-oiled cookie tin. Allow to cool completely. Store in airtight container in cool place.

brown-sugar yogurt pralines

Substitute 1½ cups light brown sugar and 1½ cups granulated sugar for 3 cups sugar.

rich pralines

Substitute 1 cup commercial sour cream for yogurt.

truffles

A favorite of continental Europe is a melt-in-the-mouth chocolate called by several names but known to most Americans as truffles. There are several ways to make them—all very easy, and all very good!

truffles

truffles

Yield: 50 ½-inch balls

> 3 1-ounce squares unsweetened
>   chocolate
> 1¼ cups sifted confectioners' sugar
> ⅓ cup margarine
> 3 egg yolks
> 1 teaspoon vanilla
> Melted chocolate, cocoa, ground
>   nuts, chocolate jimmies, or
>   coconut

Melt 3 chocolate squares over hot, not boiling, water.

Meanwhile combine sugar and margarine in mixing bowl; cream together. Add egg yolks one at a time; blend well after each addition. Stir in 3 melted chocolate squares and vanilla. Chill mixture until firm enough to handle easily. Break off small pieces; form into ½-inch balls. Roll in your favorite coating. (It is very nice to use several different coatings and arrange finished truffles in very pretty pattern on serving dish.) Allow finished balls to dry and firm on baking sheet about an hour before storing in airtight container in very cool place. These keep about a week.

If you prefer a square truffle, pour warm mixture into well-oiled 8 × 8 × 2-inch pan. Allow to cool thoroughly. Using very sharp knife, cut cooled chocolate into small squares. Coat finished squares with unsweetened powdered cocoa. An easy way to do this is to use an ordinary tea strainer as a sifter. Fill it half full with cocoa; sift very carefully over truffles. Shake off excess cocoa. If you do this on a large piece of wax paper, you can save and reuse the cocoa.

brandy or rum truffles

Yield: 35 ½-inch balls

> 1 4-ounce bar Baker's German sweet
>   chocolate
> ½ cup confectioners' sugar

> 1 tablespoon margarine
> 1 tablespoon brandy or rum
> 1 egg yolk

Melt chocolate over hot, not boiling, water.

Meanwhile cream together sugar, margarine, and flavoring.

Cool melted chocolate slightly; add to sugar mixture, stirring to blend. Immediately add egg yolk; beat until mixture is thick and creamy. Shape into ball. Cover; cool completely.

When easily handled, pinch off small piece; form into ½-inch ball. Repeat until all mixture is used. Balls can be dipped into melted chocolate, rolled in ground nuts or cocoa, or eaten as is. Can be stored about a week in airtight container in very cool place.

basic swiss-chocolate mixture (canache)

A sinfully delicious and versatile finish to a company supper.

Yield: 100 ½-inch balls

1 12-ounce package chocolate chips, melted
¾ cup whipping cream

Melt chocolate chips over hot, not boiling, water.

Heat cream in double boiler until bubbling steadily. Gradually pour cream into melted chocolate, beating vigorously with wooden spoon until dark and glossy. Return chocolate mixture to double boiler. Cook over medium heat, stirring frequently, about 25 minutes or until mixture is thick and falls heavily from spoon. Cool 5 minutes. Spread quickly in well-oiled 8 × 8 × 2-inch pan. Chill about 2 hours or until mixture is firm enough to handle easily. Cut candy into small squares or triangles, or use canapé cutters and cut into fancy, interesting shapes. You can also break off small pieces and form into ½-inch balls which can be rolled in ground nuts, chocolate jimmies, cocoa, or any coating that may strike your fancy.

1. Dip canache pieces into ground nuts.

2. Roll canache balls in chocolate jimmies.

classic hazelnut-chocolate squares

Yield: 128 ½-inch squares

1 recipe Canache (see Index)

Prepare Canache; chill in 8 × 8 × 2-inch pan.

While Canache is cooling, prepare the following:

**1 12-ounce package semisweet
    chocolate bits
1 cup finely chopped roasted
    hazelnuts (also called filberts)
¾ cup sweetened condensed milk
1 teaspoon vanilla**

Melt chocolate bits over hot, not boiling, water. Remove from heat; add nuts, milk, and vanilla. Beat gently with wooden spoon until completely blended and slightly thickened. Spread carefully over cooled Canache. Chill in refrigerator until completely cold and set. Cut with very sharp knife into ½-inch squares. Store in airtight container in very cool place. They will keep very well if kept cold, since this truffle contains no egg yolks.

basic hazelnut truffle

Prepare only the hazelnut truffle recipe. After mixture cools enough so it can be handled easily, it may be formed into ½-inch balls and rolled in your favorite coating. A delicious way to vary the coating is to roll truffle ball first in melted chocolate, then, while chocolate is still moist, roll it again in cocoa to coat. You won't have any leftovers to worry about!

caramels

Caramels are rich, chewy, and delicious. Many candy-makers have been discouraged from making them by the long and tedious process described in old cookbooks. After a little research and questioning, I found that modern candy-makers use a simple shortcut. I don't know who discovered it first, but they add the butter and cream after the syrup has reached the firm-ball stage. Making caramels in stages in this manner cuts the cooking down to a reasonable time and also makes a better-tasting candy.

wrapped caramels

34

hard caramels

hard caramels

These caramels remind me of the candy we inelegantly called "jawbreakers" when I was young!

Yield: 25 to 30

> **3 squares unsweetened chocolate**
> **3 tablespoons butter**
> **½ cup milk**
> **1 cup honey**
> **2 teaspoons vanilla**

Lightly oil inside of 2-quart saucepan. Over low heat melt chocolate and butter together in saucepan. Add milk and honey; bring to boil, stirring constantly. When mixture boils, clip on candy thermometer. Boil, without stirring, until mixture just reaches 265°F (soft-crack stage). Remove from heat immediately; add vanilla. Drop by spoonful onto very well-greased cookie tin. Allow to cool completely, then wrap each candy individually. Store in airtight container in cool place.

mocha caramels

Add 1 tablespoon instant coffee crystals to syrup as it cooks.

35

vanilla caramels

Yield: 81 1-inch pieces

2 cups sugar
1 cup corn syrup
2 cups heavy cream, lukewarm
½ cup butter
1 teaspoon vanilla

Lightly oil inside of 3-quart saucepan. Combine sugar and corn syrup in pan; cook over low heat, stirring constantly, until sugar is completely dissolved and mixture comes to boil. Clip on candy thermometer; cook, stirring occasionally, until thermometer registers 250°F (firm-ball stage). Now add warm cream very slowly, so that mixture never stops boiling. Cook until temperature reaches 250°F again. Now add butter, bit by bit, so that mixture never stops boiling. Stir a little to blend; let mixture cook to 250°F again. Remove from heat; add vanilla. Pour in steady stream into lightly oiled 9 × 9 × 2-inch pan. Do not scrape pan. Mark in 1-inch squares, but do not cut all the way through. After caramel has cooled completely, it can be turned out onto cutting board and cut into marked squares. Wrap individual pieces immediately in plastic wrap or waxed paper; store in airtight container.

butterscotch caramels

Substitute 1 cup light brown sugar and 1 cup granulated sugar for 2 cups sugar in above recipe.

chocolate caramels

Add 2 2-ounce squares bitter chocolate to sugar and corn syrup.

coffee caramels

Add 1 teaspoon instant coffee crystals to sugar and corn syrup.

nut caramels

Add 1 cup chopped nuts to syrup with the butter.

caramel-nougat roll

Substitute Basic Nougat (see Index) for fudge in Caramel-Nut Fudge Roll below.

caramel-nut roll

Use either vanilla or chocolate caramel. Allow to cool slightly. Shape into long roll about 1½ to 2 inches in diameter; roll in coarsely chopped nuts. When completely cool, cut into slices.

caramel-nut fudge roll

Prepare 1 recipe kneaded fudge; shape into long roll about 1 to 1½ inches in diameter. Pour caramel into shallow pan. When cool enough to handle, turn it out of pan onto cutting board. Cut strip large enough to wrap around fudge. Roll caramel in coarsely chopped nuts or chocolate sprinkles. Cut into slices when completely cool.

nut caramels

turtles

A party treat for children and grown-ups alike.

Yield: 60 turtles

1 pound cashew nuts
1 recipe Vanilla Caramels (see Index)
8 ounces semisweet chocolate, melted, or 1⅓ cups semisweet chocolate bits, melted

Lightly oil large baking sheet or cookie tin.

Arrange 60 groups of cashew nuts, 4 to each group.

Allow caramel syrup to cool slightly in pan, but be sure it is still liquid. Spoon tablespoon of liquid caramel over cashew nuts. Let cool 10 to 15 minutes. Spoon melted chocolate over top of each caramel turtle. Allow to cool completely until quite firm.

If you have any ingredients left over, you might want to make a few more turtles, or, pour remaining caramel into small, lightly oiled pan. Spread any remaining nuts over top; top with balance of chocolate, if any. Cut into small squares when quite cool.

Hint: If you are in a hurry and don't have time to make your own vanilla caramels from scratch, buy a 1-pound package of commercial caramels. Melt them in top of double boiler with 2 tablespoons water; use in above recipe.

pecan chews

Substitute 1 pound pecan halves for cashew nuts in above recipe. If in a hurry or run out of patience, try layering ingredients. Use well-oiled 9-inch pan. Spread layer of pecans over bottom; cover with layer of caramel syrup; top with melted chocolate. When completely cool, cut into small squares, using very sharp knife.

brittles

"Not just brittle—*peanut* brittle!" That's my husband, who has never gotten over his love affair with the goober! This is such a popular form of candy that we are lucky it is so easy to make. Just let me list a few hints to pave the way for making perfect brittles.

Always use a heavy, rather large saucepan. The sugar syrup is cooked to the hard-crack stage, and at this heat may scorch if a lightweight saucepan is used.

Adding baking soda to the syrup during the final cooking stage ensures a nice porous texture in the brittle; however, it also causes foaming, and I always use a 3-quart saucepan so the syrup won't foam over.

Despite my peanut-freak husband, I often use other nuts in making brittle. My own favorite is cashew—but, whichever kind of nuts I use, I heat them at a low temperature for about 5 minutes before adding them to the syrup. Adding cold nuts cools the syrup as it cooks. Don't roast the nuts, however; the intense heat of the syrup will roast them lightly while they cook, and preroasting could be over-roasting.

Salted or unsalted nuts? A matter of taste. I prefer unsalted nuts, but many of my friends like the contrast in taste between the sweet brittle and the salty nuts. If you prefer salted nuts, I recommend the use of very finely ground salt—about $1/8$ teaspoon per cup of nuts—mixed with the nuts before adding them to the cooking syrup.

I never attempt brittle-making on a damp day—the brittle always seems to stay sticky on a moist day. I always store it in the usual airtight container in a cool—not refrigerated—place.

peanut brittle

Yield: About 1½ pounds

    1½ cups peanuts (salted or unsalted)
    1½ cups sugar
    1½ cups light corn syrup
    ¼ cup water
    2 tablespoons margarine
    1 teaspoon vanilla
    1 teaspoon baking soda

Place peanuts in shallow pan; leave them in 200°F oven until warm, not roasted.

Lightly oil inside of 3-quart saucepan. Combine sugar, corn syrup, and water in pan. Cook over moderate heat, stirring constantly, until sugar is completely dissolved. Wipe down sugar crystals above liquid line, using clean pastry brush dipped in cold water. Let mixture come to boil. Clip on candy thermometer; cook, without stirring, until syrup reaches 270°F (soft-crack stage). Remove from heat. Add warm peanuts and margarine; stir well. Return to heat. Cook mixture, stirring frequently so mixture will not scorch, until thermometer reaches 300°F (hard-crack stage). Remove from heat. Add vanilla and baking soda; stir about 30 seconds. Mixture will lighten in color and foam. Pour syrup onto well-oiled baking tin. Jelly-roll pan is ideal, because it has sides that will prevent any spillover. I like to put the pan on a cooling rack to speed cooling and also to prevent any damage to the counter surface under the pan. Allow brittle to cool until just warm to touch; then lift whole piece with spatula. Using your hands, pull and stretch brittle as thin as you can. As it cools, you will be able to break it into small pieces. When completely cool, store in airtight container in cool, not refrigerated, place. Be sure to separate layers with plastic or waxed paper.

chocolate peanut brittle

Add 3 3-ounce squares bitter chocolate to cooking syrup.

honey peanut brittle

Substitute ½ cup honey plus 1 cup light corn syrup for corn syrup in above recipe.

lemon peanut brittle

Omit vanilla; substitute 1 teaspoon lemon extract.

almond brittle

Substitute unblanched almonds for peanuts.

walnut brittle

Substitute walnuts for peanuts.

peanut brittle

nut-toffee crunch

Toffee is much the same as super-rich brittle. The high butter content makes it a very good "keeper," and I have not found anyone yet who can resist nut-toffee crunch! You may know this candy by many names, but by any name it is the king of crunches!

Yield: 81 1-inch squares

> 1 cup lightly roasted, coarsely
>   ground or chopped almonds
> 1 cup unsalted butter
> 1 cup sugar
> ½ cup firmly packed light brown
>   sugar
> 3 tablespoons water
> ½ teaspoon baking soda
> 1 cup semisweet chocolate chips or
>   6 1-ounce squares semisweet
>   cooking chocolate, melted

Oil 9 × 9 × 2-inch pan very well. Sprinkle ½ cup almonds over bottom of pan.

Melt butter in 2-quart saucepan over low heat. Be very careful not to scorch butter. Add sugars and water. Stirring constantly, cook over low heat until sugars are completely dissolved. Let mixture come to boil. Clip on candy thermometer. Boil, stirring frequently, until thermometer registers a little more than soft-crack stage (280°F). Remove from heat. Add baking soda, stirring rapidly to blend in completely. Pour over almonds in pan; cool for a minute or two. Sprinkle chocolate bits over hot syrup; use spatula to spread chocolate that will melt from heat of syrup. If you use melted cooking chocolate, allow toffee to cool about 5 minutes, then spread melted chocolate over surface. While chocolate is still warm, sprinkle rest of nuts over surface; press down lightly. Mark 1-inch squares with edge of sharp knife while toffee is still warm. When completely cooled, break into 1-inch squares along marked lines. Store in airtight container in cool place for indefinite keeping.

deluxe topping

For an extra-special treat that turns plain ice cream into a party dessert, try crushing some Nut-Toffee Crunch (well cooled) in blender or food processor. Sprinkle over your favorite ice cream. Sensational!

nut-toffee crunch

molasses chips

These are particularly good dipped in chocolate after they are completely cool.

Yield: About 1 pound

2 cups sugar
2 tablespoons honey
2 tablespoons vinegar
2 tablespoons margarine

¾ cup water
1 teaspoon baking soda dissolved
    in ¼ cup hot water

Lightly oil inside of 3-quart saucepan. Combine sugar, honey, vinegar, margarine, and water in pan. Cook over low heat, stirring constantly, until sugar is completely dissolved. Wipe down sugar crystals above liquid line, using clean pastry brush dipped in cold water. Allow syrup to come to boil. Clip on candy thermometer. Cook over low heat, without stirring, until thermometer registers 300°F (hard-crack stage). Remove from heat. Stir in baking soda dissolved in hot water. Mixture will foam. This is a very important process, as foaming causes the honeycombing of the chips. Pour syrup onto very well-oiled baking sheet. Jelly-roll pan is ideal because shallow sides will prevent syrup from running over. When brittle is just warm to touch, cut into bite-size pieces. Store in airtight container in cool, not refrigerated, place. Will keep almost forever stored in this manner.

butterscotch brittle

Yield: About 1 pound

1 cup sugar	¼ cup water
½ cup firmly packed light brown sugar	1 teaspoon vinegar
	½ cup sweet butter*
½ cup light corn syrup	1 teaspoon vanilla

Lightly oil inside of 2-quart saucepan. Combine sugars, corn syrup, water, and vinegar in pan. Stirring constantly, cook over low heat until sugars are completely dissolved. Wipe down sugar crystals above liquid line, using clean pastry brush dipped in cold water. Let syrup come to boil. Clip on candy thermometer. Add butter in small pieces, one piece at a time, stirring constantly. Continue stirring to prevent burning; cook mixture to 300°F (hard-crack stage). Remove from heat. Add vanilla; pour onto very well-oiled baking sheet. Jelly-roll pan is ideal because low sides will keep syrup from running over. Cool until brittle is just warm to touch. Pull and stretch it as thin as you can. You can use a spatula to lift and turn warm brittle as you stretch it. Break into small pieces. When completely cool, store in airtight container in cool place. Be sure to put waxed or plastic paper between layers to keep brittle from sticking together. This candy will keep almost indefinitely stored this way.

Hint: A marvelous use for this kind of candy is as a topping. Crush brittle, using food processor, or place it in paper bag and roll it with heavy wooden rolling pin. Sprinkle pulverized brittle over ice cream or warm apple pie.

*Margarine can be substituted for butter, but for the classic flavor of butterscotch unsalted butter should be used.

sesame-seed crunch

The honey–cinnamon flavor of this typical Mediterranean-area candy conjures up memories of Mid-East bazaars.

Yield: About 1 pound

1 cup lightly toasted sesame seeds
1½ cups sugar
⅓ cup honey
2 tablespoons water
1 tablespoon lemon juice
¼ teaspoon ground cinnamon
1 tablespoon margarine

Toast sesame seeds. Place in shallow pan in 250°F oven; heat until seeds turn light-tan color. Stir frequently to prevent scorching.

Lightly oil inside of 2-quart saucepan. Combine sugar, honey, water, and lemon juice in pan. Cook over low heat, stirring constantly, until sugar is completely dissolved. Wipe down sugar crystals above liquid line, using clean pastry brush dipped in cold water. Let syrup come to boil. Clip on candy thermometer. Cook over low heat, without stirring, until thermometer registers 300°F (hard-crack stage). Remove from heat. Carefully stir in sesame seeds, cinnamon, and margarine. Pour into very well-oiled baking tin. Jelly-roll pan is ideal because low sides prevent syrup from running over. When just warm to touch, score top with sharp knife, marking 1-inch pieces. When completely cool, break crunch into pieces along scored lines. Store in airtight container in cool, not refrigerated, place. Will keep almost indefinitely stored in this manner.

nut crunch

Omit sesame seeds; substitute 1 cup of your favorite nuts, roasted lightly and either slivered or broken into small pieces.

taffy and hard candy

Have you ever read about taffy pulls? I have, and they always sounded like a lot of old-fashioned fun. With the nostalgia craze sweeping the country, it might be a lot of fun to revive the practice.

old-fashioned hard candy

old-fashioned hard candy

I have not specified the flavor or color here, as each person will have his favorite—cinnamon (use oil of cinnamon) and red, peppermint and green, lemon and yellow, and so on. If you want a variety of colors and flavors, you can carefully divide the syrup among several pans while it is still very warm, then add the flavor and color. Do not handle the syrup any more than absolutely necessary—sugar crystals tend to form very easily, and you want this candy to stay very clear and crisp.

Yield: About 1¼ pounds

    2 cups sugar
    ⅔ cup light corn syrup
    ½ cup water
    Food coloring if desired
    1 teaspoon flavoring

Lightly oil inside of 2-quart saucepan. Combine sugar, corn syrup, and water in pan. Cook over low heat, stirring constantly, until sugar is completely dissolved. Wipe down sugar crystals above liquid line, using clean pastry brush dipped in cold water. In making hard candy, it is especially important to keep these crystals from forming, so it may be necessary to wipe down inside of pan from time to time. Clip on candy thermometer. Cook syrup over moderate heat until thermometer registers 280°F (medium-crack stage). Continue boiling, but turn heat down to low point. Cook until thermometer registers 300°F (hard-crack stage). Remove from heat. Let syrup cool just a little. Stir in coloring and flavoring. Pour immediately into well-oiled 9 × 9 × 2-inch pan. As soon as cool enough to handle, but still slightly soft, cut into strips, then into small chunks. Use well-oiled scissors. Wrap each piece in plastic or waxed paper. Store in dry, cool place. If you wish, you can dust candy chunks with confectioners' sugar before wrapping.

lollipops

It is rather easy to make lollipops from above syrup. Buy wooden skewers in almost any gourmet shop or kitchenwares department. Oil large cookie tin very well. Arrange skewers in rows, being sure to leave enough space between rows for lollipops to form. When syrup is moderately cool, use tablespoon to spoon a little syrup over top of skewer. Let it to pool into a round pattie. As soon as hard enough to handle, lift pops up gently so they will not stick to pan. If you wait until they are very hard, they may crack as you lift them—hard candy becomes very brittle when cold. Wrap each lollipop separately. Store in cool, dry place. Be sure pan holding skewers is on absolutely flat surface so syrup can pool out to nice round pattie. While pops are still warm, you can decorate them—make faces, using jelly beans or gum drops; or spell out names with candy sprinkles. Again, only your imagination will limit your creativity.

honey taffy

Yield: 2 pounds

    2 cups sugar
    2 cups honey
    1 cup water
    ¼ teaspoon salt
    2 teaspoons vanilla

Lightly oil inside of 3-quart saucepan. Combine sugar, honey, water, and salt in pan. Cook over medium heat, stirring constantly, until sugar is completely dissolved and mixture comes to a boil. Wipe down sugar crystals above liquid line, using clean pastry brush dipped in cold water. Clip on candy thermometer. Let syrup boil, without stirring, until thermometer registers 280°F (medium-crack stage). Stir in vanilla. Pour syrup onto well-oiled jelly-roll pan placed on cooling rack. Let taffy cool until it can be handled comfortably, then start working it. Shape taffy into ball, then start pulling. Form long rope; double it. Redouble; pull it out again. When taffy feels light and pliable, shape into long rope about ½ inch in diameter. Using well-oiled scissors, cut into 1-inch pieces. Wrap each piece individually. Store in cool place in airtight container.

coffee and honey taffy

Add 1 teaspoon instant coffee crystals to boiling syrup for a change of taste.

half-and-halfs

Melt ½ cup semisweet chocolate bits with 1 tablespoon butter; cool. After cutting taffy into 1-inch pieces, dip one end of each piece into cooled melted chocolate. Allow about half of piece to be covered. Let chocolate dry before wrapping taffy.

molasses taffy

Yield: About 1 pound

    1 cup sugar
    ½ cup firmly packed light brown
       sugar
    1 cup light molasses
    ¼ cup light corn syrup
    ½ cup water
    1 tablespoon vinegar
    ¼ cup margarine
    1/8 teaspoon baking soda

Lightly oil inside of 3-quart saucepan. Combine sugars, molasses, corn syrup, water, vinegar, and margarine in pan. Cook over low heat, stirring constantly, until sugars are completely dissolved and mxiture comes to boil. Wipe down sugar crystals above liquid line, using clean pastry brush dipped in cold water. Clip on candy thermometer. Cook until thermometer registers 265°F (hard-ball stage). Remove from heat. Add baking soda; stir well to blend. Pour hot syrup, in slow, steady stream, onto oiled jelly-roll tin. Let syrup cool to lukewarm, then begin to work taffy with heavy spatula. Do this by pushing or working outside edge to inside until cool enough to handle. Oil your fingers well; begin pulling taffy by hand. Two people can do this together. Pull taffy into long rope, then double it over. Double it over again; pull again. Do this until it looks and feels light. Twist it into rope about ¾ inch wide; cut into 1-inch pieces with well-oiled scissors. Wrap each piece separately. Store in airtight container in cool, not refrigerated, place.

molasses mint

After syrup has cooled to lukewarm, add 5 to 6 drops oil of peppermint; continue with above method.

peppermint cushions

Yield: 1 pound

2 cups sugar
¾ cup water
2 tablespoons light corn syrup
2 tablespoons margarine
Few drops oil of peppermint or 2
    teaspoons peppermint extract

Lightly oil inside of 2-quart saucepan. Combine sugar, water, and corn syrup in pan. Cook over medium heat, stirring constantly, until sugar dissolves completely and mixture comes to boil. Wipe down sugar crystals above liquid line, using clean pastry brush dipped in cold water. Clip on candy thermometer. Boil without stirring until thermometer registers 245°F (firm-ball stage). Add margarine a little at a time so that mixture does not stop boiling. It may be necessary to stir to blend margarine into syrup. Cook syrup until thermometer registers 290°F (hard-crack stage). Remove from heat immediately. Pour at once onto well-oiled jelly-roll pan. Add flavoring; blend with heavy spatula. As soon as mixture is cool enough to handle, oil your fingers. Pull mixture into long rope; keep pulling and re-forming until mixture is opaque. Pull into long sausage shape about ¾ inches in diameter. Cut with oiled scissors, giving mixture a half turn after each cut, to form into cushion shapes—into pieces about 1 inch long. Wrap each piece separately. Store in cool, not refrigerated, place.

saltwater taffy

If you have ever vacationed at the seashore, you have probably eaten saltwater taffy. Here is the recipe to revive all your memories!

Yield: About 1¼ pounds

> 2 cups sugar
> 1 cup light corn syrup
> 1 cup water
> 1½ teaspoons salt
> 2 teaspoons glycerine (can be
>   purchased at drugstore)
> 2 tablespoons margarine
> 2 teaspoons vanilla or flavoring of
>   your choice

Lightly oil inside of 2-quart saucepan. Combine sugar, corn syrup, water, salt, and glycerine in pan. Cook over low heat, stirring constantly, until sugar is completely dissolved and mixture comes to boil. Wipe down sugar crystals above liquid line, using clean pastry brush dipped in cold water. Clip on candy thermometer. Cook without stirring until thermometer registers 260°F (hard-ball stage). Remove from heat. Add margarine. Pour hot syrup onto oiled jelly-roll tin. I like to put the tin on a cooling rack before I pour the hot syrup from the pan. This protects the surface underneath from being damaged by the extreme heat and also allows the syrup to cool faster. Let taffy cool. Add the vanilla. Begin working taffy with heavy spatula by pushing outer edges into center of taffy. When taffy is cool enough to handle, oil your fingers well; start working by hand. Gather taffy into ball; stretch into rope. Pull taffy until light in color and texture. You work it by first pulling it into long rope, then doubling and redoubling taffy, then pulling it into long rope again. Two people can do this together. When pulled enough, form into long rope about ¾ inch thick. Cut into 1-inch pieces, using well-oiled scissors. Wrap each piece separately. Store in cool place.

rainbows

A very pretty display can be made by dividing cool taffy into several small balls. Tint each with a different color. Be very careful to add just a drop or two of coloring at a time so that tints remain a subtle pastel. You can match color to flavor, such as yellow with lemon, green with mint, orange with orange, and pink with cinnamon or mint. For variety try almond flavoring instead of vanilla with white taffy. Wrap each candy in clear plastic wrap so that the color shows through. Use a large glass bowl full of taffy for an unusual and edible party centerpiece.

candied fruits and nuts

Have you seen the sign that says "We buy junk, we sell antiques"? The same principle can be applied to throw-aways, in this case thick-skinned grapefruit or orange rinds. With just a little more than a wave of a wand—voila!—a fairy-princess candy from scraps. After the first of the year, when thick-skinned grapefruits and oranges abound, I scoop out and serve the fresh sections for breakfast. Instead of throwing away the rinds, I wrap them in plastic wrap and save them in the refrigerator until I have the rinds from 3 grapefruits or 6 oranges. They keep well in the refrigerator for several days. Of course, if you have a large family to feed, you will have enough after one meal. For a lovely color try to use at least one ruby-red grapefruit.

apricot "paper"

apricot "paper"

When my children were young, one of their favorite confections was something that, for lack of a better name, they called apricot "paper." It was a very thin sheet of sweet, pureed apricots, chewy and delicious. It came rolled into a cone shape, wrapped in plastic wrap. For years I did not see it for sale, then when I came across it once more, this time in a specialty shop, it was terribly expensive. With a little effort and a lot of cooperation from mother nature, you can make this treat. Once made and wrapped, it will keep indefinitely.

Yield: 2 large sheets about 12 × 36 inches; recipe can be halved

**8 cups small pieces very
    ripe apricots
¾ cup sugar
A promise of 3 consecutive
    days of warm sunshine!
A table that can be placed
    outside in the sun, out of reach
    of inquisitive animals
Clear plastic wrap, very heavy
    quality**

Combine apricots and sugar in large saucepan or heavy pot. Cook over low heat until mixture comes just to boiling point. Do not boil. Using blender or food processor, process fruit, a little at a time, until completely pureed. Let puree cool to lukewarm.

Meanwhile prepare your setup. Place table where it will get maximum full sunlight. Place plastic film on table—cut it into convenient lengths to handle; it usually comes in 12-inch widths. Place pieces side by side on table; weight corners if necessary. When fruit puree is lukewarm, pour a puddle into center of each sheet of plastic; spread it with spatula to about ¼ inch thick. To be sure flies do not get into fruit, tent large piece of cheesecloth over top of table. You can do this by putting a tall bottle in center of table, draping cheesecloth over it, fastening it under edges of table with tape. Dry in direct sunlight 3 days. After first day puree will be firm enough that you will be able to slip cookie tin under plastic film. Carry sheets of apricot puree inside for the night. Place in sunshine next day. After three days of sun-drying, you will be able to pull apricot "paper" from plastic. Roll it into cones or cylinders; wrap each in plastic wrap. To eat, just tear pieces off, take a taste, and let nature take its course!

This might sound like a lengthy procedure, and it is. But children love to help in the preparation, and it can be a fun, family project.

candied grapefruit or orange rind

Yield: About 1 pound

> Rind from 3 grapefruits or
>   6 oranges
> Water
> Salt
> ½ cup water
> 2½ cups sugar
> Granulated sugar

Using your fingers, pull out all membrane and some of soft white inner rind; leave some, however. This is a matter of experience and judgment, and it is impossible to tell you exactly how much white inner rind to leave. Cut rind into even strips about ⅛ inch wide. You should have about 6 or 7 cups of rind strips. Place in large saucepan; add enough cold water to cover well. Measure water as you add it. Add 2 tablespoons salt per quart of water. Bring to boil; boil gently 20 minutes. Drain rind well. Cover again with cold water—do not add salt—and bring to boil. Cook gently 15 minutes. Drain; repeat step again. Drain well. Add ½ cup water and 2½ cups sugar; heat slowly, stirring enough to dissolve sugar. Bring to boil; cook slowly until all syrup is absorbed and rind looks clear. This may take as long as an hour, but it really needs no attention while slowly cooking, and you can do other things meanwhile.

Spread large baking tin with sugar. When rind is done, take few strips at a time and roll them in sugar.

Heat oven to 250°F, then turn off heat. Place pan of sugared rind in oven; leave overnight to dry. This candied rind will keep indefinitely stored in airtight container in cool place.

Note: This recipe can be doubled.

chocolate candied rind

If you wish to dip candied rind in chocolate, roll finished candied rind in confectioners' sugar instead of granulated sugar; omit oven drying. Cool strips, then dip.

holiday candied rind

You might want to tint candied rind in appropriate colors for holiday celebrations—red for Christmas or a variety of pastels for Easter. It is easy to tint the sugar that the rind is rolled in by adding a few drops of color directly to the granulated sugar and shaking it in a jar. Be sure to add color gradually so you do not over-color.

fruit and nut ball

Prunes or dates, pitted and stuffed, are a wonderful confection, providing an endless variety of tastes, limited only by your imagination. Buy them already pitted, or remove the stones yourself, using a sharp knife to slit the fruit, but being very careful not to cut them all the way through. Stuff the cavity with Fondant (see Index); dip in melted chocolate or try any or all of the following.

Yield: 3 cups mixture, about 48 ½-inch balls

1 cup dried figs	Grated rind of 1 orange
1 cup pitted dates	1 tablespoon lemon juice
1 cup walnuts	Confectioners' sugar

Using fine blade of grinder or food processor, grind together figs, dates, and walnuts. Add orange rind, lemon juice, and just enough confectioners' sugar to bind all together into paste. Form small balls; use to stuff dates or prunes, or use as is. Roll stuffed fruit or fruit and nut ball in confectioners' sugar. Allow to air-dry 2 or 3 hours before storing. Store in airtight container in refrigerator 3 to 4 weeks.

apricot ball

Substitute 1 cup dried apricots for figs.

spice balls

Add ½ teaspoon cinnamon and ¼ teaspoon nutmeg to fruit and nut mixture.

sugared nuts

Serve with coffee at the end of a meal for a very sophisticated finish.

Yield: 1 pound

1 pound shelled walnut halves	½ cup water
1½ cups sugar	1 teaspoon vanilla

Lightly toast walnuts (see Index—Nuts); set aside.
Lightly oil inside of 2-quart saucepan. Combine sugar and water in pan. Cook over medium heat, stirring constantly, until sugar is completley dissolved and mixture comes to boil. Wipe off sugar crystals above liquid line, using clean pastry brush dipped in cold water. Clip on candy thermometer. Cook without stirring until thermometer registers 238°F (soft-ball stage). Remove from heat. Stir in nuts and vanilla. When nuts are coated, turn out onto lightly oiled baking tin; separate. Cool completely. Serve.

variation

You can substitute any of your favorite nuts for walnuts, but try to use either whole or perfect halves.

coffee nuts

Add 1 teaspoon instant coffee crystals to water.

orange nuts

Omit vanilla; add 1 tablespoon orange-flavored liqueur with nuts.

sherried nuts

Substitute sherry for water.

spiced nuts

Add ½ teaspoon cinnamon and ¼ teaspoon nutmeg when nuts are added.

spiced nuts

marron glacé

Everyone knows that the French have a very special way with food—their desserts and confections are world renowned. These are worth the time and trouble.

Yield: 1 pint marron glacé

1 pound chestnuts, blanched	1 cup water
2 cups sugar	1 teaspoon vanilla

To shell and blanch chestnuts, cover with boiling water; simmer gently about 20 minutes. Cool just enough to handle; peel with sharp knife. Leave peeled chestnuts whole; if tender, you can use them as is. If not completely tender, cover with fresh boiling water; simmer very gently until tender.

Combine sugar and water; cook over medium heat, stirring constantly, until sugar is completely dissolved. Wipe down sugar crystals above liquid line, using clean pastry brush dipped in cold water. Continue boiling, without stirring, until sugar begins to turn slightly golden. Remove from heat. Add vanilla. Carefully place chestnuts in syrup; leave them 5 mintues. Remove carefully to rack to dry. I use small tongs for this. Save syrup. Let chestnuts dry overnight. Following day heat syrup just to boiling point. Remove from heat. Place chestnuts in syrup; leave them 5 minutes, then remove them; let dry again. At this point they can be used in any recipe calling for marron glacé; or, with vanilla ice cream, make a delicious dessert. They can be eaten plain, as you would any confection. If you are not going to use them immediately or have some left over to save, place in jar. Pour boiling syrup over chestnuts. Store in refrigerator. They will keep a long time.

Chopped marron glacé mixed with freshly whipped cream makes a perfectly marvelous filling for cream puffs or layers of sponge cake.

brandied marron glacé

For the grown-ups in the family, add 3 tablespoons brandy to basic syrup after it has been removed from heat. Proceed as above.

rum marron glacé

Instead of brandy use 3 tablespoons rum to flavor basic syrup; proceed with rest of recipe.

glacé fruit

Not as sugared as candied fruit, glacé fruit makes a beautiful and elegant way to finish a meal.

glacé syrup

1 cup sugar
½ cup water
3 tablespoons light corn syrup

Lightly oil inside of 2-quart saucepan. Combine sugar, water, and corn syrup in pan. Cook over moderate heat, stirring constantly, until sugar is completely dissolved and mixture comes to boil. Wipe down sugar crystals above liquid line, using clean pastry brush dipped in cold water. Clip on candy thermometer. Boil fairly rapidly until thermometer registers 290°F (hard-crack stage). Remove from heat immediately. Have ready fruit you wish to dip and cooling rack on which to cool fruit. Dip each piece quickly into hot syrup; place on rack to dry. These should be used within few hours of cooling for finest taste.

fruit

Clusters of grapes—a variety of
    colors is beautiful
Fresh strawberries
Fresh cherries
Sections of oranges or tangerines
Pineapple

Wash and dry each piece of fruit thoroughly. Allow moist fruit such as orange sections to air-dry at least 2 hours before dipping.

ginger candies for passover (ingberlach)

Yield: 50 to 60 pieces

2 cups honey
1 cup sugar
2 cups coarsely chopped walnuts
2 cups matzo farfel
1 teaspoon ground ginger

Lightly oil inside of 3-quart saucepan. Combine honey and sugar in pan; cook over low heat, stirring constantly, until sugar is completely dissolved. Bring mixture to boil; cook until syrup is golden brown. Remove from heat at once. Add nuts, farfel, and ginger. Pour onto wet board; immediately spread to square about ½ inch thick. You can use a spatula, or, with great care, use your fingers, first dipping them into ice water to keep from burning. Cut candy into 1-inch squares while still warm. Store in airtight container in cool place.

carrot ingberlach

Substitute 2 cups finely grated carrots for farfel in above recipe. Cook carrots with honey and sugar.

sesame squares

Yield: About 30 2-inch squares

2 cups toasted sesame seeds
1½ cups honey
1 tablespoon lemon juice

Lightly oil inside of 3-quart saucepan. Combine sesame seeds, honey, and lemon juice in pan. Cook to boiling point over medium heat. Clip on candy thermometer; cook, stirring, to 280°F (soft-crack stage). Pour immediately onto well-greased jelly-roll tin; sides will prevent mixture from running over. As it cools, you can coax edges into an even shape. When cool, cut into 2-inch squares or 2 × 4-inch bars. This will be quite chewy. Wrap each piece in waxed paper or plastic wrap. Store in airtight container.

Note: This candy becomes "brittle" if cooked to 300°F. After it cools, it can be broken into small pieces and stored in an airtight tin. Remember, moisture is the enemy of brittles!

sesame bars

halvah

Halvah is a Middle-Eastern favorite. My husband and I have always loved this ancient confection, so I was both surprised and delighted when I discovered how easy it is to make at home. Sesame seeds can be found in almost any health-food store, and sesame oil is sold in Oriental grocery stores. I prefer making halvah in a food processor, but a blender can be used.

Yield: 128 ½-inch pieces

> **3 cups unhulled sesame seeds**
> **1 teaspoon sesame oil, or as little as**
>   **needed**
> **7 tablespoons honey (½ cup less 1**
>   **tablespoon)**
> **1 tablespoon vanilla**

Place sesame seeds in blender or food processor. Blend at highest speed (if using food processor, process with steel blade) until seeds form a paste. Add sesame oil; if seeds seem very oily, you may not have to use all the oil, so be sure to add just a drop or two at a time. Continue blending. Add honey and vanilla; blend well. Press mixture (will be very firm) into 8 X 8 X 2-inch pan; chill. When thoroughly chilled, cut into ½-inch squares.

almond halvah

Substitute 2 teaspoons almond extract for 1 tablespoon vanilla in above recipe. Add ½ cup toasted almonds to finished halvah.

chocolate halvah

Add 1 square melted semisweet chocolate to above recipe as it is being blended.

marble halvah

Divide finished halvah into two portions. Add ½ square melted semisweet chocolate to one portion; mix well. Spoon into pan, alternating flavors; blend, using spatula.

pistachio halvah

Pistachio nuts are particularly good with halvah. For a very special treat knead ½ cup pistachio nuts into finished halvah.

poppy-seed candy (mohneleck)

Yield: 40 to 50 1-inch pieces

> 1 pound poppy seeds
> 2 cups honey
> ½ cup sugar
> 2 cups coarsely chopped pecans
> ¾ teaspoon ground ginger

Wash poppy seeds in hot water. Drain well; dry between paper towels. Grind in food grinder, or process a few seconds in food processor. If you have neither, you can pound seeds with a pestle to crush them. Poppy seeds left whole do not have the good flavor that crushed seeds have.

Lightly oil inside of 3-quart saucepan. Combine honey and sugar in pan; cook over low heat, stirring constantly, until sugar dissolves and boiling point is reached. Add poppy seeds; cook until thick, stirring frequently so mixture will not scorch. This candy is difficult to test with a thermometer, so you will have to use your judgment to determine when it is done. You can test by dropping spoonful onto wet board. If it holds its shape, proceed. Add nuts and ginger; stir well. Cook another minute or so, until nuts are heated through. Turn mixture onto thoroughly wet board. Pat mixture into square about ½ inch thick. You can use large spatula, or, if very careful, dip your hands into ice water and pat with wet fingers. After candy has cooled about 10 or 15 minutes, cut into 1-inch squares, using very sharp knife. You can dip knife into hot water to make it easier to cut. Store in airtight container in cool place.

grandma's nut candy (noent)

Yield: 50 to 60 pieces

> 2 cups honey
> ½ cup sugar
> 4 cups walnuts

Lightly oil 3-quart saucepan. Mix honey and sugar together in pan; cook over low heat until boiling point is reached. Boil, without stirring, 10 minutes. Add nuts; cook until candy thermometer registers 272°F (soft-crack stage). Turn out immediately onto wet bread board; mixture will be very thick. Pat into square about 1 inch thick. You can use a spatula, or, if very careful, dip your hands into ice water first to keep them from burning, and use your fingers. Cool until you can touch candy with your bare hands. Cut into squares with very sharp knife.

This is a brittle-type candy and must be stored in an airtight container.

pecan chew

Substitute pecans for walnuts.

divinity and nougat

Divinity is a marvelous, light, very old-fashioned candy. Making it brings back such vivid memories of my childhood that I can smell and almost feel my mother's kitchen. However, I must give you a few warnings. Do not try to make divinity on a damp, rainy, or snowy day—or on a very warm day. Those are the times to make a foolproof fudge! Unless your beating arm is very strong, I would recommend the use of an electric mixer—portable, if that is what you have, but a stationary, table-top mixer is really the easiest and best to use. If you must beat by hand, try to have a helper available so that one person can beat while the other pours the hot syrup into the egg whites.

Read the directions carefully, and assemble all ingredients and utensils you will need before you start. Remove the eggs from the refrigerator, and separate the whites from the yolks while the eggs are cold; it is much easier to separate cold eggs. However, warm egg whites beat to a much larger volume than cold egg whites, so allow the whites to come to room temperature before using. Cover and refrigerate the yolks to use in another recipe. This might be a good time to consider making chocolate truffles; only the egg yolks are needed for this confection.

Divinity keeps almost forever, but it must be stored in an absolutely airtight container in a cool place. It picks up moisture from the air and becomes very sticky, so take out only as much as you expect to use immediately.

divinity

basic divinity

The flavor of divinity, like most candy, improves after a day or two of ripening. My helpers have to be satisfied with licking bowls and spoons and the promise of the real thing later!

Yield: 36 to 50 pieces

½ cup water
½ cup light corn syrup
2 cups sugar
¼ teaspoon salt
2 egg whites
1 teaspoon vanilla
½ cup chopped nuts

Lightly oil inside of heavy 2-quart saucepan. Combine water and corn syrup in pan. Cook over moderate heat until mixture boils. Remove from heat. Add sugar and salt. Cook over moderate heat, stirring constantly, until sugar is completely dissolved. Cover; cook until mixture comes to boil. Uncover immediately. Clip on candy thermometer. Cook over medium heat, *without stirring*, until thermometer registers 260°F (hard-ball stage).

Begin beating egg whites while syrup is cooking—the object is to have syrup reach 260°F about same time egg whites are beaten very stiff. I start beating egg whites at about time syrup reaches soft-ball stage; it usually goes fairly rapidly after that point. Beat egg whites very stiff.

As soon as syrup has reached 260°F begin pouring it over beaten egg whites *with mixer still running.* This is why stationary electric mixer is so important in divinity-making. Recruit your helper at this point if you don't have an electric mixer. Pour syrup in slow but steady stream. Add vanilla at some point during mixing; beat until divinity is quite thick and loses its glossy look. It will hold its shape when dropped from tip of spoon when it is ready. Add nuts very quickly. Drop by spoonful onto well-oiled cookie tin. Work as rapidly as possible, so divinity does not cool down in bowl. Store in absolutely airtight container in cool place.

fruit divinity

Follow directions for Basic Divinity. Add ½ cup raisins or ½ cup of any chopped candied fruit. For very festive look, use ½ cup chopped candied cherries.

honey divinity

Omit corn syrup in Basic Divinity recipe; substitute ½ cup honey.

maple divinity

Add ½ cup pure maple syrup to water and corn syrup in Basic Divinity recipe.

orange divinity

Add 2 or 3 teaspoons grated orange rind to basic recipe. For very special orange divinity also add ¼ cup chopped candied orange rind while beating.

peppermint divinity

Omit nuts and vanilla from Basic Divinity; substitute 1 teaspoon peppermint flavoring. One-half cup crushed peppermint candy can be added to mixture while beating.

chocolate divinity

Yield: 50 pieces

    ½ cup water
    ½ cup light corn syrup
    1 cup firmly packed light brown
        sugar
    1 cup granulated sugar
    2 1-ounce squares unsweetened
        chocolate
    ⅛ teaspoon nutmeg
    2 egg whites
    1 teaspoon vanilla
    ½ cup semisweet chocolate bits

Lightly oil inside of heavy 2-quart saucepan. Combine water and corn syrup in pan. Cook over moderate heat until mixture boils. Remove from heat. Add sugars, chocolate squares, and nutmeg. Cook over moderate heat, stirring constantly, until sugars are completely dissolved and chocolate is melted. Wipe down sugar crystals above liquid line, using clean pastry brush dipped in cold water. Cook without stirring until mixture boils. Wipe down sugar crystals again. Clip on candy thermometer. Cook over moderate heat to 260°F (hard-ball stage).

Begin beating egg whites before syrup is finished cooking, so egg whites will be beaten stiff and syrup will have reached 260°F about same time. I start when softball stage is reached. Beat egg whites very stiff. Keep mixer going or enlist the aid of a friend. Pour chocolate syrup in steady stream over egg whites. Add vanilla while beating. When mixture is quite thick and has lost its glossy look, stir in chocolate bits. Working rapidly, drop by spoonfuls onto well-greased cookie sheet. Store in absolutely airtight container in cool place. Try to keep tasters away for a day or two so flavor can ripen.

mocha divinity

Serve these with hot, fragrant espresso for an elegant finish to dinner.

Yield: 50 pieces

½ cup strong black coffee or ½ cup
    water and 2 teaspoons instant
    coffee
½ cup light corn syrup
1 cup firmly packed light brown
    sugar
1 cup granulated sugar
¼ teaspoon salt
2 1-ounce squares unsweetened
    chocolate
2 egg whites
1 teaspoon vanilla
½ cup chopped nuts

Lightly oil inside of heavy 2-quart saucepan. Combine coffee and corn syrup in pan. Cook over moderate heat until mixture boils. Remove from heat. Add sugars, salt, and chocolate. Cook over moderate heat, stirring constantly, until sugars are completely dissolved and chocolate is melted. Wipe down sugar crystals above liquid line, using clean pastry brush dipped in cold water. Cook without stirring until mixture boils. Wipe down sugar crystals again. Clip on candy thermometer. Cook over moderate heat, *without stirring*, until mixture reaches 260°F (hard-ball stage).

Begin beating egg whites before syrup is quite finished so egg whites will be beaten stiff and syrup will reach 260°F about same time.

When syrup reaches 260°F, pour over egg whites in steady stream with beater still running. If attempting this without electric mixer, try to have someone help at this stage; it is almost impossible to beat and pour at same time. Add vanilla while mixing; beat until mixture is quite thick and no longer glossy. Stir in nuts. Drop by spoonfuls onto well-oiled cookie sheet. Store in absolutely airtight container in cool place. Try to keep from sampling for a day or two so flavor can ripen fully.

basic nougat

After you have mastered divinity, you might want to try your hand at making nougats. This is an old-fashioned candy, and not easy to make, but chewy and delicious. Sometimes it's fun to meet the challenge of a difficult recipe! An electric mixer is an absolute must. Please read the directions carefully, as nougat is made in two stages.

Yield: About 60 pieces

> 1½ cups sugar
> ½ cup light corn syrup
> ½ cup water
> 1 egg white
> 2 teaspoons vanilla
> 2 tablespoons melted margarine
> 1 cup lightly roasted almonds,
>   slivered
> ½ cup diced, candied cherries
> Cornstarch for coating

Lightly oil inside of 2-quart saucepan. Combine sugar, corn syrup, and water in pan. Cook over low heat, stirring constantly, until sugar is dissolved. Wipe down sugar crystals above liquid line, using clean pastry brush dipped in cold water. Cover saucepan; let syrup boil 2 minutes. Remove cover; wipe down sugar crystals again, if necessary. Clip on candy thermometer. Cook syrup over low heat, without stirring, to 238°F (soft-ball stage).

When syrup is almost at soft-ball stage, start beating egg white in bowl of electric mixer. When syrup reaches 238°F, with mixer running at highest speed, pour ½ of syrup over egg white. Beat until very thick; let stand.

Return other half of syrup to heat. Cook until it reaches 275°F (just a little past soft-crack stage).

Start mixer again. Pour hot syrup over egg–syrup mixture in bowl; beat until very thick. It will be very heavy. Test for doneness by taking a little mixture out with spoon. If it holds its shape and doesn't feel sticky, it is ready for pan. Blend in vanilla, margarine, nuts, and cherries. Spread in oblong pan about 9 × 5 × 2 inches that has been well oiled, then dusted lightly with cornstarch. Let cool overnight, but do not place in refrigerator. Traditional shape for nougats is about ¾ × 1 inch. Please cut carefully with sharp knife or scissors dipped into cold water. If you want to dip these pieces into chocolate, it should be done at this stage. Otherwise, wrap each piece in plastic or waxed paper. Store in airtight container in cool place. They will keep a long time this way.

confetti nougat

Omit nuts and cherries; substitute 1 cup small gumdrops.

dark nougat

Substitute light brown sugar, tightly packed, for granulated sugar.

confetti nougat

fondant and marzipan

Fondant is a versatile sweet that can be used for centers, for coating, or for layering in bars or candy logs. It can be stored in bulk in an airtight container in a cool place for weeks and can be used as you need it.

Traditionally, marzipan, an almond-fondant candy, has been used for molding into all sorts of fanciful shapes for parties, especially at holiday time, for special sweet decorations. If you have a great deal of patience to combine with your imagination, you can form all kinds of vegetables and fruits, wreaths and baskets, bread and rolls. You can buy molds for shaping marzipan or you can mold the shapes you want by hand, using unbeaten egg white or corn syrup for "glue" and a very fine artist's brush for "painting."

fondant mints with pastel-tinted white chocolate coating

basic uncooked fondant I

Yield: 1¼ pounds

    4 cups confectioners' sugar
    3 tablespoons milk
    1 tablespoon margarine
    1 egg white
    1 teaspoon vanilla

Combine all ingredients; mix until smooth and easily handled. If mixture is too stiff, add a few drops of milk. Form into ball. Place in tightly covered container. Let mellow at least an hour before using. Store in airtight container.

basic uncooked fondant II

Yield: 1½ cups

    1 1-pound box confectioners' sugar
    ¼ cup light corn syrup
    1 egg white
    Flavoring
    Food coloring
    Confectioners' sugar for dusting board and rolling pin

Combine all ingredients; mix well until mixture holds together. Turn out onto board dusted with confectioners' sugar; knead several minutes, until no longer sticky. Add any desired flavoring and/or coloring. Roll to ½ inch thick with wooden rolling pin that has been dusted with confectioners' sugar. Cut into any shape you like; tiny canapé cutters can be used to get unusual shapes. Roll leftover fondant into small balls. Place all finished pieces on cookie rack to dry several hours. Store in airtight container in cool place.

fruit fondant

Add 2 tablespoons any fruit-flavored powdered drink mix to basic fondant; knead until well blended. These mixes are usually colored, so you do not have to add additional coloring.

peppermint fondant

Add 5 or 6 drops oil of peppermint to basic fondant; knead as directed.

maple-cream fondant

Spring is always maple-syrup time in New England and one of my favorite times to visit my Boston children. I always promise myself I will not get on the return plane looking like a pack rat—but there I am, unable to get up the aisle without bumping my various parcels and shopping bag on each seat, hoping it will all stow under the seat in front of me! One of my prizes, always, is "real" maple syrup to be used on our favorite French toast—and—made into confections, the very smell of which recalls the Vermont woods.

Yield: 1 pound

> 2 cups sugar
> ¾ cup water
> ⅔ cup pure maple syrup (other syrup
>   will not do)
> 1 teaspoon vanilla

Lightly oil inside of 3-quart saucepan. Combine sugar, water, and maple syrup in pan. Stirring constantly, cook over low heat until sugar is completely dissolved. Wipe down sugar crystals above liquid line, using clean pastry brush dipped in cold water. Cover pan; let mixture come to boil. Uncover pan; wipe down sugar crystals again. Clip on candy thermometer. Cook without stirring to 240°F (soft-ball stage plus about 1 minute of cooking). Remove from heat immediately. Pour in slow but steady stream onto large baking tin or cookie sheet oiled lightly or wet with cold water. Do not scrape pan. I like to put the baking sheet on a cooling rack before pouring the fondant so the mixture will cool evenly and the surface under the pan will be protected from burning. Cool to 110°F (lukewarm). Add vanilla. Work fondant by lifting and folding cooled syrup. When mixture begins to "whiten," oil your hands. Gather into ball by kneading gently. Store in airtight container; let mellow overnight before using. Use, as you wish, for centers, for coating, or for layering in bars or candy logs.

creamy maple-cream fondant

Add 2 tablespoons margarine as you work fondant.

maple-nut fondant

Add 1 cup chopped walnuts as you work fondant.

maple-raisin fondant

Add ½ cup chopped raisins to fondant as it is worked.

basic cooked fondant

Yield: 1¼ pounds (enough for about 100 small centers)

3 cups sugar	1 tablespoon light corn syrup
1½ cups water	1 teaspoon vanilla

Lightly oil inside of 3-quart saucepan. Combine sugar, water, and corn syrup in pan. Stirring constantly, cook over low heat until sugar is dissolved. After sugar is dissolved, wipe down sugar crystals above liquid line, using clean pastry brush dipped in cold water. Let syrup come to boil. Cover with tight lid for 2 minutes to allow steam to wash down sugar crystals; uncover. Cook, without stirring, to 240°F (soft-ball stage, plus 1 minute of cooking). Remove from heat. Pour in steady rather slow stream onto baking sheet or cookie tin either lightly oiled or wet with cold water. Do not scrape pan. I like to put the baking sheet on a cooling rack so the fondant can cool evenly and the surface under the tin will be protected from burning. If you have marble slab, pour hot syrup onto slab wet with cold water. Cool to 110°F (lukewarm). Add vanilla. Begin working fondant by lifting and folding cooled syrup. Mixture will become white instead of clear as you work it. Oil your hands at this point; knead until smooth and creamy and holds together. Gather into ball. Store in airtight container. It should be allowed to mellow overnight before using.

coffee fondant

Omit water; use 1½ cups strong coffee. Or add 2 teaspoons instant coffee concentrate to water.

cream fondant

Follow above recipe; add 2 tablespoons margarine as fondant is worked.

fruit fondant

Add 1 cup chopped candied cherries, pineapple, or other candied fruit as fondant is worked. Do not add fresh or moist fruit of any kind; it will cause fondant to liquify.

lemon or orange fondant

Omit vanilla; add 5 or 6 drops oil of lemon or orange for strong flavor or 1 teaspoon lemon or orange extract for slightly milder flavor. Do not add grated peels; this will cause fondant to liquify.

maple-nut fondant

Omit vanilla; add 1 teaspoon maple extract and ½ cup chopped walnuts.

marzipan fondant

Omit vanilla; add 1 teaspoon almond extract and ½ cup finely chopped or ground almonds.

penuche fondant

Use 1½ cups granulated sugar and 1½ cups firmly packed light brown sugar instead of 3 cups granulated sugar.

rum-raisin fondant

Omit vanilla; add 1 teaspoon rum extract and ½ cup chopped raisins.

fondant kisses

Yield: 50 to 100 kisses

¾ cup shredded or grated coconut
1 tablespoon confectioners' sugar
1 teaspoon vanilla
Coloring (optional)
1 recipe Basic Fondant (see Index)

Mix coconut and confectioners' sugar together. Knead coconut, vanilla, coloring, and fondant together. Break off small piece, about level tablespoonful; shape into ball or crescent. Repeat until fondant is all used. Place finished shapes on large cookie tin; let air-dry overnight. To store, either wrap each piece separately and store in airtight container or layer with piece of waxed paper between layers to keep kisses from sticking to each other.

chocolate-cream patties

1 recipe Chocolate-Cream Fondant (see Index)

Follow method for shaping Peppermint Patties (see Index). After drying, chocolate-cream patties can be dipped in chocolate or in Fondant Coating (see Index).

chocolate fondant

Yield: 1¼ pounds

　　3 cups sugar
　　1½ cups water
　　1 tablespoon light corn syrup
　　2 1-ounce squares unsweetened
　　　　chocolate
　　1 teaspoon vanilla

Lightly oil inside of 3-quart saucepan. Combine sugar, water, corn syrup, and chocolate in pan. Stirring constantly, cook over low heat until sugar and chocolate are completely melted. After mixture is thoroughly blended, wipe down sugar crystals above liquid line, using clean pastry brush dipped in cold water. Let mixture come to boil; do not cover. When mixture boils, wipe down sugar crystals again. Clip on candy thermometer. Boil without stirring to 238°F (soft-ball stage). Remove from heat. Pour in slow but steady stream onto either marble slab or wet large cookie sheet that has been placed on cooling rack. Placing baking sheet on rack will allow mixture to cool evenly, since air can circulate around it; will also protect surface under it from burning. Cool to 110°F (lukewarm). Add vanilla. Begin working fondant with heavy spatula. When fondant thickens, oil your hands; knead gently until it forms a ball. Place fondant ball in airtight container; let mellow overnight before using.

chocolate-brandy fondant

Omit vanilla; add 1 teaspoon brandy extract.

chocolate-cherry fondant

Omit vanilla; add 1 teaspoon cherry flavoring and ½ cup chopped candied cherries. Do not use moist cherries; that will cause fondant to liquify.

chocolate-cream fondant

Follow above recipe; add 2 tablespoons margarine as fondant is worked.

chocolate-mint fondant

Omit vanilla; add 6 or 7 drops mint oil or 1 teaspoon mint extract.

chocolate-nut fondant

Add 1 cup chopped walnuts as fondant is worked.

chocolate-rum fondant

Omit vanilla; add 1 teaspoon rum extract.

chocolate rum-raisin fondant

Omit vanilla; add 1 teaspoon rum flavoring and ½ cup chopped raisins.

mocha fondant

Omit vanilla; add 1 teaspoon instant coffee concentrate to water.

peppermint patties

Yield: 1¼ pounds

> 1 teaspoon peppermint extract or
> 8 to 10 drops peppermint oil
> 1 recipe Basic Fondant (see Index)
> Confectioners' sugar

Knead flavoring into fondant. Form round balls about size of a walnut. I flatten these balls into round patties by using a water glass with a perfectly flat bottom.

Sift a little confectioners' sugar onto small plate. Dip bottom of water glass into sugar; press down firmly on top of ball of fondant. Lift carefully. Sugar will keep glass from sticking. With a little practice you will be able to make uniform patties about ½ inch thick. Let these air-dry 1 hour. Dip in chocolate according to Chocolate Dipping directions (see Index).

basic marzipan

Yield: Enough to mold about 30 pieces of fruit

    1 8-ounce can almond paste or 1 cup
        Food-Processor Almond Paste
        (see Index)
    4 tablespoons margarine
    2 teaspoons light corn syrup
    ½ teaspoon almond extract
    2 tablespoons cherry-flavored
        liqueur (optional)
    2½ cups sifted confectioners' sugar
    Food coloring for tinting

Combine almond paste, margarine, and corn syrup together until smooth. Add almond extract and cherry liqueur; blend. Divide coloring into equal portions for tinting: ⅓ white, ⅓ red, ⅓ green, for instance. Divide sugar into same portions. Blend coloring and sugar into paste. Wrap each portion separately in waxed paper; refrigerate. You can use any coloring appropriate for the shapes you intend to make. You can add a little confectioners' sugar if it is needed to produce firm marzipan. Marzipan can be stored in airtight container in refrigerator for several weeks and used as needed.

chocolate marzipan rolls

Make cylinders about 1 inch long from marzipan. Dip end, covering about ½ of cylinder, into melted semisweet chocolate.

marzipan flowers

Tint marzipan pale pink and pale yellow. Mold tiny petals from each color. Using drop of corn syrup, glue one petal to next at base.

marzipan fruit

Using yellow marzipan, roll small lemon shapes. Make rough marking by pressing against finest grater. Use whole clove or nutmeg, stuck into end, for stem. Following same procedure, you can mold oranges, strawberries, peaches, etc. just by varying color in marzipan and shape of fruit.

marzipan-stuffed fruit

Remove pits from dates and prunes; stuff centers with small balls of marzipan. Use variety of colors to make rainbow dessert plate.

74

marzipan leaves

Tint marzipan medium green. Mold tiny ovals; flatten into leaf shapes. Using toothpick, make vein markings. Attach to base of flowers with drop or two of corn syrup.

marzipan vegetables

Start with mushrooms—be sure to vary size for a "real" look. Caps are flattened balls with little dusting of cocoa on flat bottoms. Roll tiny cylinders for stems; attach with drop or two of corn syrup. Only your supply of marzipan and your imagination will stop you now! Potatoes are made with rather heavy dusting of cocoa and few "eyes" made with end of toothpick.

Hint: If you want, you can paint the marzipan shapes, using a fine artist's brush and vegetable coloring. Allow shapes to air-dry at least 2 or 3 hours before attempting any surface coloring.

chocolate marzipan rolls

food-processor almond paste

Yield: About 2 cups

    1½ cups blanched almonds, unroasted
    ¾ cup sugar
    2 tablespoons water
    1 tablespoon lemon juice

Follow directions for your particular food-processor for grinding nuts or, using blender, grind almonds very, very fine.

Combine sugar, water, and lemon juice in small saucepan. Cook over medium heat, stirring constantly, until sugar is dissolved and syrup comes to boil. Boil exactly 5 minutes without stirring. With food-processor running and ground almonds in processor container, pour hot syrup into spout; run until just blended. Remove paste; form into ball. Place in tightly covered container; allow to mellow in refrigerator 3 or 4 days. Use as called for in the marzipan recipe.

If using blender to grind almonds, remove ground almonds to mixing bowl. Pour hot syrup over almonds, mixing well; proceed as above.

marshmallows and
jelly candies

If you think marshmallows come only two ways—large and mini—and from supermarket shelves—think again! With an electric mixer, an absolute necessity for making marshmallows, since it takes about 15 minutes of hard beating to produce the fluffy candy we all love; very simple ingredients; and a lot of imagination you can make very tasty, wholesome marshmallows with a lot of pizzaz.

Marshmallows are an incredible candy to have fun with. Start with any of the basic or flavored marshmallows. Cut 1-inch squares, and stick a sturdy toothpick into the center of one side, leaving about half of the toothpick sticking out. Dip the other end into melted chocolate. Use these mini-marsh pops to decorate a child's birthday cake or individual cupcakes. Make them even fancier—dip the melted chocolate into multicolored candy sprinkles while the chocolate is still warm!

Instead of cutting squares, cut fancy shapes, using very sharp cookie or canapé cutters. Dip into tinted coconut—for instance, a chick marshmallow dipped into yellow-tinted coconut makes an edible Easter favor.

Mix leftover bits of marshmallow and melted chocolate with a few roasted nuts. Drop from the end of a spoon onto a well-oiled cookie tin, allow to dry for an hour or two, and you have delicious candy bites.

To make ice-cream topping, melt marshmallows in a well-oiled saucepan with a teaspoon or two of liquid added. Use water, fruit juice, or flavored liqueurs for the adults.

Nothing beats hot chocolate with one or two marshmallows melting on top for a warm-up drink after a spell of snow-shoveling or ice-skating. Sometimes we even indulge after a lazy afternoon!

basic uncooked marshmallows

Yield: 128 ½-inch or 64 1-inch marshmallows

2 envelopes unflavored gelatin (2 tablespoons)
⅓ cup cold water
½ cup sugar
⅔ cup light corn syrup
1 teaspoon vanilla
¼ cup confectioners' sugar combined with ¼ cup cornstarch

Combine gelatin and cold water in small saucepan. Let mixture stand about 5 minutes or until firm. Place over hot water; stir until gelatin is completely dissolved. Liquid will be clear and syrupy. Add sugar to warm mixture; stir until sugar is dissolved. Pour syrup into large bowl of electric mixer. Add corn syrup and vanilla; beat on highest speed 15 minutes, until very light and fluffy.

Lightly oil 8 × 8 × 2-inch pan; sprinkle bottom with half of confectioners' sugar and cornstarch mixture. Pour marshmallow mixture into pan; smooth top to even out. Let marshmallow cool overnight in refrigerator. Sprinkle rest of confectioners' sugar and cornstarch over top. Loosen sides with spatula; lift out entire piece. Place on cutting board. I cut this large piece of marshmallow into 1-inch pieces with scissors that I dip in cold water. There will be a lot of loose confectioners' sugar and cornstarch left in the pan and on top of the marshmallow. I roll each small marshmallow in this mixture, then put them on a cooling rack to dry for an hour or two. Can be stored in airtight container and will stay nice and moist at least 3 weeks.

chocolate-covered marshmallows

basic cooked marshmallows

Yield: 64 1-inch or 128 ½-inch marshmallows

    2 envelopes unflavored gelatin
        (2 tablespoons)
    ½ cup cold water
    2 cups sugar
    ¾ cup light corn syrup
    ¾ cup water
    2 teaspoons vanilla
    ¼ cup confectioners' sugar mixed
        with ¼ cup cornstarch

Combine gelatin and ½ cup cold water in large electric-mixer bowl. Let mixture stand while you prepare sugar syrup.

Lightly oil 2-quart saucepan. Combine sugar, corn syrup, and ¾ cup water in saucepan. Cook over medium heat, stirring constantly, until sugar dissolves. Cover; bring to boil. Remove cover as soon as mixture boils; cook, without stirring, to 245°F (firm-ball stage). Remove from heat. Attach electric beater; with mixer beating, pour hot syrup slowly into softened gelatin. Entire process should take about 15 minutes. Add vanilla at very end of beating process. At this point marshmallow mixture should be very light and fluffy.

Lightly oil 8 × 8 × 2-inch pan. Sprinkle half the confectioners' sugar–cornstarch mixture over bottom; pour marshmallow mixture over this. Chill overnight in refrigerator. When ready to cut marshmallows, sprinkle rest of confectioners' sugar–cornstarch mixture over top of marshmallow. Lift entire piece out of pan onto cutting board. I use very sharp scissors, dipped into cold water periodically, to cut marshmallow into 1-inch pieces. Roll pieces in confectioners' sugar–cornstarch mixture; you will have enough left in bottom of pan for this step. Let marshmallows dry on cooling rack an hour or two. Store in airtight container. They will stay moist at least 3 weeks.

chocolate marshmallows

Follow either Basic Marshmallow recipe; add 2 squares unsweetened chocolate, melted and cooled, to marshmallow during beating step.

toasted-coconut marshmallows

Instead of using confectioners' sugar and cornstarch to coat marshmallows, sprinkle pan with 1 cup lightly toasted coconut. After marshmallow mixture has cooled, sprinkle top with 1 cup lightly toasted coconut. After marshmallows are cut to desired size, roll each piece in coconut that has fallen off.

fruity marshmallows

Substitute fruit juice for water when softening gelatin.

Important note: Do not use fresh pineapple juice; it will prevent marshmallows from jelling. You can use canned pineapple juice, however, or cook fresh juice before using.

fruit and nut marshmallows

Add 1 cup of your favorite candied fruit, chopped nuts, dates, figs, or raisins after marshmallow is beaten and before it is spread to cool.

minty marshmallows

Omit vanilla; substitute few drops oil of peppermint or 1 teaspoon peppermint extract.

marshmallow crispies

Yield: 96 1-inch squares

¼ cup margarine
4 cups tightly packed marshmallows
6 cups crisp rice cereal

Melt margarine in 3-quart saucepan. Add marshmallows; cook over low heat, stirring constantly. When marshmallows are completely melted, add rice cereal; stir just until all blended. Immediately press mixture into well-oiled, shallow pan about 12 × 9 inches. When cool, cut into 1-inch squares.

chocolate-chip marshmallow crispies

Add 1 cup semisweet chocolate chips to rice cereal.

nutty marshmallow crisp

Add 1 cup chopped walnuts to rice cereal.

peanut-freak marshmallow crispies

Add ½ cup peanut butter to marshmallows as they are melting. You can use either chunky or smooth-style. For true peanut freak add ½ cup peanuts with rice cereal.

lollies

Instead of pressing marshmallow mixture into pan, mold warm mixture into 2-inch balls. Stick wooden skewer into each ball to make lollipop. Decorate with jimmies, jelly beans, or any other small candies. They make marvelous party candy for children.

deccos

Instead of cutting cooled mixture into squares, use sharp cookie cutters and make any shape that pleases you.

marshmallow crispies

wicked temptation

wicked temptation

Now that you have a batch of delicious homemade marshmallows, what is more natural than to combine them with nuts and chocolate for this tempting treat?

Yield: 128 ½-inch pieces

> 1 pound semisweet or milk chocolate
> 1 cup lightly toasted pecans or walnuts
> 1 recipe Basic Marshmallows (see Index)

Melt chocolate in top of double boiler over hot, not boiling, water. Stir until chocolate is smooth. Pour ½ of chocolate into very well-oiled 8 × 8 × 2-inch pan. Sprinkle nuts and marshmallows over chocolate. Pour rest of chocolate over nuts and marshmallows. Cool until firm; cut into small pieces. Will keep almost indefinitely stored in cool place in airtight container.

basic fruit jellies

Jelly candies are a first cousin to marshmallows. These are very good on their own and, layered with marshmallow, make a pretty, tasty, special treat.

Yield: 64 1-inch pieces or 128 ½-inch pieces

basic jelly-candy syrup

3 envelopes unflavored gelatin
    (3 tablespoons)
2 cups sugar
1 cup water
6 drops yellow food coloring
    (optional)

¼ cup orange juice plus grated
    rind of 1 orange
2 tablespoons lemon juice plus
    grated rind of 1 lemon
Granulated sugar for coating

Combine gelatin, sugar, and water in 2-quart saucepan. Heat over medium heat, stirring constantly, until mixture boils. Boil slowly 20 minutes. Remove from heat.

Add coloring, orange juice and rind, and lemon juice and rind to syrup; stir 2 or 3 minutes.

Oil 8 × 8 × 2-inch pan. Strain hot mixture into pan; chill in refrigerator until very firm. Turn entire piece onto well-oiled baking sheet—you may have to use a spatula. Cut into pieces of desired size by pressing very sharp knife down into jelly. Do not cut by drawing knife through—this will spoil shape of pieces. Roll each piece in granulated sugar to coat. Let dry several hours on cooling rack. Store in airtight container. Jellies will stay very nice and moist at least 2 weeks.

orange-liqueur fruit jellies

For grown-up candy-eaters try substituting ¼ cup of any orange-flavored liqueur for rinds in above recipe.

layered candies

Yield: 64 1-inch pieces or 128 ½-inch pieces

1 recipe Basic Jelly-Candy Syrup (see Index)
1 recipe Basic Marshmallows (see Index)
Granulated sugar for coating

Prepare Basic Jelly-Candy Syrup. Pour ½ into well-oiled 8 × 8 × 2-inch pan; put into refrigerator to firm. Leave remainder in pan, at room temperature.

After refrigerated jelly has set, prepare Basic Marshmallow recipe; spread carefully on top of set jelly. Try to keep layer even. Pour remainder of syrup over marshmallow layer. If syrup has begun to set, warm it very briefly to liquify, but do not let it get hot as it will melt the marshmallow when poured over that layer. Chill in refrigerator overnight. Loosen jelly by running spatula around sides. Turn out onto well-oiled baking pan. Cut by pressing very sharp knife down through jelly and marshmallow, but do not try to cut by drawing knife through candy. Roll each piece in granulated sugar; let dry several hours before storing. Store in airtight container.

jellies rolled in powdered sugar

mint jellies

Yield: 64 1-inch pieces or 128 ½-inch pieces

**3 envelopes unflavored gelatin
(3 tablespoons)
2 cups sugar
1½ cups water**

**6 drops green coloring (optional)
¼ teaspoon oil of peppermint
Granulated sugar for coating**

Combine gelatin, sugar, and water in 2-quart saucepan. Heat over medium heat, stirring constantly, until mixture boils. Boil slowly 20 minutes. Remove from heat. Add coloring and flavoring.

Oil 8 × 8 × 2-inch pan. Pour hot mixture into pan; cool in refrigerator until very firm. Turn entire piece onto well-oiled baking sheet—you may have to use a spatula. Cut into desired-size pieces by pressing very sharp knife down into jelly. Do not try to cut by drawing knife through; this will spoil shape of pieces. Roll each piece in granulated sugar; dry on cooling rack several hours before storing. Store in airtight container. Will stay very nice and moist at least 2 weeks.

creme de menthe jellies

For grown-up candy eaters try substituting ¼ cup creme de menthe for oil of peppermint.

jellies rolled in granulated sugar

spice jellies

Yield: 64 1-inch pieces or 128 ½-inch pieces

**3 envelopes unflavored gelatin
(3 tablespoons)
2 cups sugar
1½ cups water
6 drops red coloring
¼ teaspoon oil of cloves
Granulated sugar for coating**

Combine gelatin, sugar, and water in 2-quart saucepan. Heat over medium heat, stirring constantly, until mixture boils. Boil slowly 20 minutes. Remove from heat. Add coloring and flavoring.

Oil 8 × 8 × 2-inch pan. Pour hot mixture into pan; cool in refrigerator until very firm. Turn piece onto well-oiled baking sheet; you may have to use spatula. Cut into desired-size pieces by pressing very sharp knife into jelly. Do not try to cut by drawing knife through—this will spoil shape of pieces. Roll each piece in granulated sugar; dry on cooling rack several hours before storing. Store in airtight container in cool place. Will keep about 2 weeks.

popcorn

Of course you can buy already popped corn, but what fun is that? It isn't necessary to have a corn-popper, but, if you do, by all means use it. If not, improvise with a very heavy saucepan and lid. Buy very good-quality popping corn. You'll get much better results, and the difference in cost is very little.

popcorn

popcorn

Use good-quality salad oil—it will stand high temperature without smoking or burning, and it has a neutral flavor. Cover bottom of 5-quart saucepan with shallow layer of oil—not much is needed. Heat oil over moderately hot fire. Drop in 3 or 4 kernels of corn; when they pop, add layer of corn to cover bottom of pan. Cover, with lid only partly on pan. Object is to allow steam to escape and to keep in popping corn. When corn begins to pop, shake pan to keep corn moving so it doesn't burn. When you can't hear anymore kernels popping, it will be finished and you can put it into a large bowl to cool. If you want plain popcorn, this is it. If you want salted, buttered, cheesed, or candied corn, this is the point at which you add other ingredients.

Note: 1 cup unpopped kernels will produce 4 to 5 cups popcorn. Be sure to pick out and discard any unpopped kernels before serving or using in other recipes.

buttered popcorn

Mix ¼ cup melted butter with 4 to 5 cups popped corn. Toss; serve.

cheese popcorn

Mix ¼ cup finely grated cheese—any hard cheese you like can be used—with 4 to 5 cups hot popped corn. Toss so corn will be coated with cheese.

garlic popcorn

Mix together ¼ teaspoon garlic powder, ¼ teaspoon seasoned salt, and ¼ cup melted butter. Toss with popcorn. This makes an unusual and very good garnish for creamed soups.

herbed popcorn

Mix together ¼ teaspoon dried parsley, ¼ teaspoon dried oregano, ¼ teaspoon seasoned salt, and ¼ cup melted butter. Allow mixture to stand about an hour before using, so flavors will blend. Toss through popcorn. (Or use any combination of any of your favorite herbs.)

salted popcorn

Add light sprinkling of salt; toss through popcorn.

caramel syrup

Yield: 1 cup

> ½ recipe Vanilla Caramels (see Index)
> ¼ cup water

Lightly oil inside of small saucepan. Combine caramels and water in pan. Heat over medium heat, stirring enough to combine water and caramels. When caramels are completely melted, pour hot syrup over warm popcorn. Mix to coat popcorn completely. When cool enough to handle, form into 2- to 3-inch balls.

chocolate-caramel syrup

Use Chocolate Caramels (see Index) in place of Vanilla Caramels, or add 1½ squares (1½ ounces) unsweetened chocolate to above.

marshmallow syrup

Yield: About 2 cups

> 4 cups marshmallows, tightly packed
> ¼ cup melted margarine

Lightly oil inside of small saucepan. Combine marshmallows and margarine in pan. Stirring constantly, heat over low heat until marshmallows are completely melted and syrup is hot. Pour over 9 to 10 cups warm popcorn; mix well so popcorn is completely coated. When just cool enough to handle, form into balls about 2 to 3 inches in diameter.

confection syrup

Yield: About 1½ to 2 cups, enough to coat 9 to 10 cups popcorn or rice cereal

> 2 cups sugar
> 1¼ cups water
> 2 tablespoons light corn syrup
> 1 tablespoon margarine
> 1 teaspoon vanilla

Lightly oil inside of 2-quart saucepan. Combine sugar, water, and corn syrup in pan. Cook over medium heat, stirring constantly, until sugar is completely dissolved and syrup boils. Wipe down any sugar crystals above liquid line. Clip on candy thermometer. Cook over medium heat, without stirring, until thermometer registers 270°F (soft-crack stage). Remove from heat. Stir in margarine and vanilla. Pour hot syrup at once over popcorn or rice cereal; stir to blend. When just cool enough to handle, form into 2- to 3-inch balls.

candy popcorn balls

Yield: 15 to 20 popcorn balls

    9 to 10 cups popped corn
        (2 cups unpopped kernels)
    Syrup of your choice

Keep popped corn in warm place while you make syrup. Pour hot syrup over warm corn; stir to coat popcorn completely. While corn is still very warm, but cool enough to handle, oil your hands very well. Form small balls 2 to 3 inches in diameter. Place finished balls on oiled cookie tin to cool. Wrap each ball individually in plastic wrap; store in cool place. If well-wrapped, it is not necessary to put them into airtight container. I use a large freezer bag to store wrapped popcorn balls.

chocolate-chip popcorn balls

Add 1 cup semisweet chocolate chips to popcorn before adding syrup.

confetti popcorn-ball confections

Add 1 cup chopped candied cherries to popcorn before adding syrup.

fruit and nut popcorn balls

Add 1 cup raisins or chopped dried fruit and 1 cup lightly roasted nuts to popcorn before adding syrup.

peanut 'n popcorn balls

Add 1 cup lightly roasted peanuts to popcorn before adding syrup.

popcorn party plans

Let your imagination run wild! Candy popcorn can be molded into almost any shape you desire—or put together to make all kinds of decorations.

For edible *Christmas-tree decorations,* cut 6-inch lengths of fancy ribbon or string. Double over to form 3-inch loop. Mold warm Candy Popcorn Balls (see Index) around cut ends of string, leaving closed loop with which to hang popcorn balls. If you want extra color, vegetable coloring can be added to syrup before forming balls.

For *party swags,* cut ribbon or twine in lengths you wish to use. Staple loop of molded popcorn balls (see above) to ribbon at 4- to 6-inch intervals.

Instead of making popcorn balls, warm popcorn plus syrup can be pressed into well-oiled pan; cut into bars when cool. Or, press mixture into shallow pan; cut into fancy shapes with very sharp cookie cutters. These are especially good for children's parties.

You can make a *snowman* to use for a centerpiece by molding 3 graduated-size balls. Put together with largest ball on bottom, middle size in center, and smallest on top. Use small candies or gumdrops for eyes, nose, mouth, and buttons. Children will be delighted!

When my children were away at camp or school, they looked forward to "care packages" from home. Instead of using paper filler to ensure against breakage, I always used plain unbuttered, unseasoned popcorn. On arrival this edible filler can be reheated, seasoned to taste, and enjoyed. It makes a party out of every package!

confections

There may be an honest difference of opinion about whether certain sweets are candy or cookies, so I compromise by calling them confections.

I never throw away anything that can be used, even if it has to be disguised! This is true for all kinds of stale bread, rolls, cake, and cookies. The bread and rolls go into the food-processor to become crumbs with endless uses. I take off any soft icing from stale cake and discard that. Then, again, into the food-processor, grinder, or blender to become crumbs. Keep flavors separate. You can store crumbs in jars in the refrigerator and use them as needed. Cookies can be crumbled as is. Nuts, raisins, chocolate chips, or dry sugar add to the flavor. I do try to keep chocolate and vanilla separate. Obviously, the flavor of the crumbs you use will affect and change the flavor of the confection you are making, but by all means don't be afraid to change and experiment.

coconut drops

Yield: About 48

    ½ cup semisweet chocolate
        bits or 3 ounces (3 squares)
        semisweet chocolate
    2 tablespoons margarine
    2 cups confectioners'
        sugar, sifted
    2⅔ cups flaked or
        shredded coconut
    ½ cup instant dry milk
    1 teaspoon vanilla

Melt chocolate and margarine over warm, not boiling, water. Blend in remaining ingredients. Drop by spoonful onto well-oiled cookie tin. Let harden at least 1 hour before storing. Store in airtight container in cool place.

black bottoms

Melt chocolate; set aside. Blend remaining ingredients; drop by spoonful onto well-oiled cookie tin. Let dry about ½ hour. Dip bottom of each piece of candy into melted chocolate. Turn upside down to dry. Store in airtight container in cool place.

butterscotch goodies

Substitute butterscotch bits for chocolate in above recipe; proceed according to directions.

peanut angels

Substitute ½ cup peanut bits for chocolate. Melt with margarine; set aside.
Blend remaining ingredients together. Drop by spoonful onto well-oiled cookie tin. Let dry about ½ hour. Dip bottom of each piece of candy into melted peanut candy. Turn upside down to dry. Store in airtight container in cool place.

brandy balls

These are especially popular at holiday time.

Yield: 48 1-inch balls

1 cup semisweet chocolate chips
  (1 6-ounce package)
1 small can evaporated milk
  (5 ounces)

2½ cups cookie crumbs
½ cup confectioners' sugar, sifted
1 cup coarsely chopped pecans
⅓ cup brandy

Combine chocolate chips and milk in 2-quart saucepan. Cook over low heat, stirring constantly, just until chocolate is melted and mixture well blended. Remove from heat.

Combine remaining ingredients; add to melted-chocolate mixture, mixing well. Cool about ½ hour. Shape mixture into small balls about 1 inch in diameter. Finished balls can be rolled in confectioners' sugar, cocoa, candy sprinkles, ground nuts, or flaked coconut. For a very pretty tray of brandy balls, use a variety of coatings. Let finished brandy balls air-dry an hour or two, then store in airtight container in refrigerator. Be sure to bring to room temperature before serving.

raisin–rum balls

Soak ½ cup seedless raisins in ⅓ cup rum; drain well. Use rum in place of brandy in recipe as directed. Form balls with several raisins in center. If you want a shortcut, just mix raisins right into other ingredients.

brandy balls

rum balls

rum balls

Yield: 36 1-inch balls

  **1 cup cookie crumbs, chocolate or
    vanilla
  1 cup confectioners' sugar
  1½ cups finely chopped walnuts
  2 tablespoons light corn syrup
  4 tablespoons rum
  2 tablespoons cocoa**

Combine cookie crumbs, sugar, 1 cup walnuts, corn syrup, rum, and cocoa; mix well. Form into 1-inch balls. Roll each ball in reserved walnuts. Air-dry about 1 hour. Store in airtight container in cool place. Will keep several weeks.

variations

Garnish each finished ball with ½ candied cherry or ½ walnut pressed into top.

Reduce nuts to 1 cup. Roll finished balls in sugar or shredded coconut.

97

cornflake crunch

Yield: 81 1-inch squares

2 cups cornflakes	¼ cup firmly packed dark brown
1 cup crisp rice cereal	sugar
1 cup coarsely chopped roasted	2 tablespoons margarine
walnuts	1 teaspoon vanilla
¾ cup light corn syrup	

Combine cereals and nuts in large mixing bowl; set aside.

Lightly oil inside of 2-quart saucepan. Combine corn syrup, sugar, and margarine in pan. Cook over medium heat, stirring constantly, until mixture comes to full boil. Boil 3 minutes, stirring to prevent scorching. Remove from heat; cool 10 to 15 minutes. Add vanilla; beat with wooden spoon until mixture lightens and thickens. Pour over cereal and nuts; mix thoroughly. Press warm mixture into well-oiled 9 × 9 × 2-inch pan. When completely cool and firm, cut into 1-inch squares.

Note: For a taste change vary the flake cereal you use; however, always include 1 cup crisp rice cereal. Do not use sugar-coated flakes.

chocolate-chip crunch

Add ½ cup semisweet chocolate chips to cereal and nuts.

mocha crunch

Add ½ cup semisweet chocolate chips to cereal. Add 2 teaspoons instant coffee crystals to syrup as it cooks.

kisses

Under any name these melt-in-the-mouth morsels are irresistible!

Yield: 60 to 70 kisses

2 egg whites	½ cup sugar
⅛ teaspoon salt	1 tablespoon brandy
⅛ teaspoon cream of tartar	4 or 5 drops orange bitters

Be sure egg whites are at room temperature so you will get maximum volume when beating. Place egg whites in mixing bowl of electric mixer. Add salt and cream of tartar; beat at high speed until egg whites are very foamy and beginning to thicken. Add the sugar a little at a time, beating very well after each addition. Sugar should be as dissolved as possible. It is impossible to beat this too much. When egg whites are very stiff, add brandy and orange bitters. Drop by teaspoonful onto very well-oiled cookie tins. Bake at 300°F 25 minutes. Turn off oven; open door a little to allow oven to cool slowly. Leave kisses in oven until cool. They will be very dry and crisp. Remove from pans. Make sure they are completely cool, then store in airtight container.

almond kisses

Add 1 cup thinly sliced or coarsely ground unblanched, roasted almonds to meringue mixture with brandy and orange bitters.

chocolate-chip kisses

Add 1 cup semisweet chocolate chips with brandy and orange bitters.

choco-peppermint kisses

Omit brandy and orange bitters; add 4 or 5 drops of oil of peppermint and 1 cup chocolate chips.

coconut clusters

Add 1 cup shredded or flaked coconut to meringue mixture with brandy and orange bitters.

peppermint kisses

Omit brandy and orange bitters; add 4 to 5 drops oil of peppermint. Tint light green with few drops of food coloring.

chocolate-chip kisses

taffy apples

Halloween just isn't Halloween for me without candy apples. Luckily, apples are at their best and least expensive in the fall, and that is when I am most likely to indulge the children in the family—and some of the grown-ups, too—with this delicious treat.

Yield: 8

> **8 large firm apples**
> **8 wooden skewers**
> **2 cups sugar**
> **¾ cup water**
> **¼ cup light cream**
> **2 tablespoons light corn syrup**
> **2 tablespoons margarine**
> **1 teaspoon vinegar**

Wash and dry apples. Insert wooden skewer into end of each apple; set aside.

Lightly oil inside of 2-quart saucepan. Combine remaining ingredients in pan. Cook over low heat, stirring constantly, until sugar is completely dissolved. Wipe down sugar crystals above liquid line, using clean pastry brush dipped in cold water. Bring mixture to boil. Clip on candy thermometer. Cook over low heat, without stirring, until thermometer registers 260°F (hard-ball stage). Remove from heat.

Holding apple by end of skewer, dip it into hot syrup, twirling it around and allowing syrup to cover apple completely. As soon as apple is completely covered with hot syrup, plunge it into bowl of cold water; remove it immediately. Place on well-oiled cookie tin to harden completely. Plunging apple into cold water cools syrup abruptly and keeps it from pooling when apple is placed on cookie tin to cool. If syrup begins to thicken before you are finished, reheat it just enough to liquify it. These taffy apples do not keep longer than about 24 hours.

Drop any leftover syrup by spoonful onto oiled cookie tin to make small, hard candies.

Note: This syrup is very hot and should be handled with caution. I like an adult to do the actual dipping and the children to assist with plunging the apples into cold water.

nut or coconut taffy apples

While taffy is still warm, dip end of apple into crushed nuts or grated coconut.

cinnamon taffy apples

Add few drops red coloring and oil of cinnamon to taffy syrup after it has reached 260°F and you have removed it from heat.

caramel apples

Yield: 8

8 large firm apples
8 wooden skewers
1 recipe Vanilla Caramels (see Index)
1 tablespoon water

Wash and dry apples. Insert wooden skewer into end of each apple; set aside.

Oil inside of 2-quart saucepan. Melt caramels and water together, or make 1 recipe of caramels and use while hot. When caramel is hot, hold apple by end of skewer; dip apple into hot caramel. Twirl around so entire apple is coated. Allow excess to drip back into pan. Place apples on well-oiled cookie tin to dry and harden. If caramel begins to thicken too much before you are finished dipping all the apples, reheat it over very low heat. Wrap individually; these apples will become very sticky if left at room temperature without wrapping.

Any leftover caramel can be poured into small, well-oiled pan to harden; cut into 1-inch squares. Wrap individually to keep them from getting sticky.

variations

While apples are still warm, dip ends into crushed nuts or grated coconut.

party suggestion

While caramel coating is still sticky, apples can be turned into funny faces. Use shredded coconut for hair, hard candies or gum drops for eyes, nose, and rosy cheeks. A thin strip of orange rind makes a mouth.

For Halloween use candy corn to make "pumpkin" faces on apples.

For Christmas you can use shredded coconut for hair and a Santa beard. Raisins and chocolate chips make good eyes, and a nose from a candied cherry is perfect!

dipping, coating, and icing

chocolate dipping

Don't be afraid to dip! Do be sure you are well organized before you start and that you are using coatings and centers that will work together. Try to get the weather to cooperate—or make your own by using your air conditioner. Most of all—relax! Remember that practice really does make perfect and that even less than perfect first attempts will be eaten with enthusiasm by your family. Leftovers are never a problem—just use them in making more candy!

The making of chocolate, beginning with a bean from the cacao tree that is cleaned, roasted, crushed, heated, and processed, is a complex and very exotic story. We take for granted the finished product—chocolate—in its various forms, flavors, and degrees of sweetness. We can buy chocolate in bulk, ranging in flavor from unsweetened to milk, usually in 10-pound cakes sold by suppliers or in the more familiar 8-ounce packages, each ounce wrapped separately. Chocolate chips in either milk or semisweet form are also available, of course, but I do not recommend using chocolate chips for dipping purposes. If you are going to be dipping a large amount of chocolates, it will be practical to buy the chocolate in 10-pound cakes; otherwise, use any good cooking chocolate, either semisweet or unsweetened, found on grocery shelves. It is not practical to work with less than 1 pound of chocolate at a time, however, so be sure to start with 2 packages of 1-ounce pieces. Read the label carefully; be sure you do not use chocolate with vegetable shortening added—cocoa butter is the essential ingredient in chocolate to be used for dipping. German's sweet chocolate comes in 4-ounce bars and makes a marvelous sweet coating. The degree of sweetness in the coating is a matter of taste; however, usually, the sweeter the center, the less sweet the coating should be. I don't like to use completely bitter chocolate for the coating—if I want it to be virtually unsweetened, I use 1 or 2 ounces of semisweet chocolate to every 6 ounces of unsweetened. However, I have friends who really like a very bitter chocolate coating, so I always save some centers to dip in unsweetened chocolate.

It is very important to control the temperature of chocolate while it is being heated and also while it is being cooled. Never try to dip chocolates on a warm, humid day unless your kitchen is air-conditioned. Water is the enemy of chocolate. Even one drop of water in the melted chocolate being used for coating can cause streaking in the finished candy. This is also caused by the tendency of cocoa butter to separate from the other ingredients and show up as gray streaks when the candy cools. This is why it is so important to store candy in a cool place, so that repeated melting and hardening won't occur.

Before you start to work, organize your area. You must have enough room to set up your assembly line—centers to be dipped, a marble or formica slab for dipping, and a tray lined with waxed paper on which to put the finished candy. Do not use an oiled or greased pan; dipped chocolates will pick up the oil.

Chocolate to be melted must be grated or broken into small pieces first so it will melt evenly. If you have a food-processor, use it. Do not use a blender; it will start the melting process in the blender, and you will not have an evenly heated product with which to work. If you must hand-grate, use a large square grater, so that the grated chocolate falls into a bowl through the center of the grater. I suggest this because I have found that when I use a flat grater, flakes of chocolate fly all over the place, making a mess.

Place grated chocolate in top of small double boiler; set aside.

Fill bottom of double boiler with enough water so that when top is put in place, water comes almost to bottom of top pan, but doesn't quite touch. Heat water to 140°F—use a candy thermometer to test temperature. Turn off heat. Place top pan with grated chocolate in it over water; stir continuously, mashing chocolate against sides of pan to help it melt. As soon as chocolate is completely melted, remove top pan from double boiler; continue stirring chocolate vigorously. Let water in bottom cool to 110°F. This will happen fairly fast. Replace top pan over bottom pan; stir once in a while to keep chocolate uniform in consistency. As you use chocolate, water in bottom pan might cool off too much. Replace it with warm water from faucet. If unsure of temperature, test again with candy thermometer. Like so many things we do, experience provides us with confidence, but, until you can judge temperature yourself, rely on your thermometer. When you change water, be sure to put chocolate aside—far aside. You don't want one drop of water to get into melted chocolate.

After replacing chocolate over warm water, you are ready to dip. Use one hand for working; be sure to keep one hand clean and dry for picking up centers and decorating. With working hand scoop up 2 or 3 handfuls melted chocolate; put it on dipping surface. Needless to say, surface must be clean and completely dry before you start to work. Use working hand to move melted chocolate into pool about 4 or 5 inches wide; keep working chocolate around and around until it cools to about 89°F. This is less then body temperature, but still warm. If you want to check carefully to see what 89°F feels like, cool pan of water to this temperature before you start working; put your fingers into it. To test further, a few drops of melted chocolate will harden on piece of waxed paper in about 1½ minutes if at proper temperature. Using clean hand, pick up a center—or whatever you are going to dip— and drop it into melted chocolate. At this point you can use either dipping fork or two of your fingers formed into a V. Practice making the "V-for-victory" sign, and you will have correct finger position. The dipping fork is not really a fork but more of a circle and can be purchased at specialty shops or from commercial suppliers. Your fingers are always available and with some practice will become very dexterous. With fingers, cover center completely with melted chocolate; allow excess to drip back into pool: You can help this along by holding candy in your fingers with your palm up and gently rapping back of your hand against slab. Give the covered center a little twist so top has squiggle or swirl of chocolate on it. Professionals use a code so that each piece is marked with a designation that tells what the center is. Until you are adept enough to do this, I would suggest keeping centers that are alike together; when finished, label your storage boxes appropriately.

Pool of chocolate you are dipping into will cool rapidly; when it does, scrape up cooled chocolate and return to double boiler to remelt.

With working hand place dipped candy on waxed paper; leave it in same position to harden. Do not move chocolates around until quite firm, or you will have very messy-looking pieces of candy.

With clean hand you can decorate finished candy, if you wish, with chocolate sprinkles, nut halves, chocolate shot, or any other topping.

If your first dipped candies are less than beautiful, turn them into "French" chocolates by rolling in ground nuts or chocolate sprinkles while chocolate coating is still slightly soft. This will cover a multitude of mistakes and allow you to practice, and you will still have nice-looking candies to serve to guests or family.

A wide variety of centers can be dipped in chocolate. These include fondant, both cooked and uncooked. Allow fondant centers to age at least 2 days before dipping, or they will leak through chocolate bottoms. All fudge is doubly delicious when dipped. You can dip nougat, toffee, marshmallows, jellies, caramels, divinity, truffles, any confections in this book, dried fruits, lightly roasted nuts, pretzels, cookies, crackers, and fresh fruit. When dipping fresh fruit, allow it to air-dry before dipping; plan to serve it the same day. My grandchildren especially love bananas dipped in chocolate. A most elegant dessert is a fondue pan filled with dipping chocolate, kept warm over pan of water. Provide dinner guests with plates of fresh fruit and fondue forks; allow them to dip their own. The last of the chocolate can be mopped up with pieces of sponge cake!

After dipping centers, if you have leftover chocolate, mix in nuts, raisins, coconut, bits of marshmallow, or combination of these. Drop by teaspoonful onto waxed paper; allow to dry. There is no waste in making candy!

chocolate-covered nougat and marzipan balls

fancy chocolate lollipops dipped in multicolored candy sprinkles

chocolate-dipped pretzels summer coating

105

cordial cherries

One mystery of dipped chocolates always intrigued me. How did the liquid around cherries or pineapple get into the chocolate case? When I was a child, I had visions of someone injecting the liquid into the candy with a hollow needle! Actually, there is no real mystery. The answer lies in the reaction between the fruit, a mixture of chemicals you can buy in the drugstore, and fondant plus a chocolate coating.

Yield: 50

cordialing mixture

½ ounce grain alcohol	½ ounce 8% acetic acid
½ ounce glycerine	1 ounce distilled water

Have your druggist mix the above, or buy the ingredients and mix them together yourself.

50 maraschino cherries	Fondant Coating (see Index)
1½ cups Fondant (see Index)	Dipping Chocolate (see Index)
½ teaspoon Cordialing Mixture	

Drain cherries completely. After they are drained, wipe surface of each cherry dry; place on rack to air-dry. Just before dipping, dust very lightly with confectioners' sugar.

Melt fondant and cordialing mixture together in top of double boiler. Dip cherries just as any other center, using Fondant Coating. Place on waxed paper to dry. As soon as Fondant Coating has hardened, dip in chocolate just as you would any center. As soon as chocolate has hardened, *dip again,* so coating will be rather thick. This is to prevent leakage of the cordial. Allow to harden; set aside at least 12 hours. Cordialing mix will combine with fondant and very slight moisture remaining in center of cherry to liquify and produce the lovely cordial center we all love.

variations

Substitute small pieces of candied pineapple or several raisins for maraschino cherry.

brandy cherries

Use candied instead of maraschino cherries. Soak overnight in enough brandy to cover. Drain cherries completely; reserve brandy for other uses. Follow procedure for dipping maraschino cherries. Instead of brandy, you can use rum or any cherry-flavored liqueur.

stemmed cherries

Use maraschino cherries with stems still attached. Follow same procedure as for de-stemmed cherries; do not cover stem. Hold cherry by stem to dip in fondant, then in chocolate. It is easier to dip this kind of cherry, as it has a built-in handle!

chocolate-dipped cherries

chocolate easter egg

Chocolate chips, melted, 6 ounces per 6-inch egg
½ recipe Basic Decorating Icing (see Index)
Small Chocolate Leaves for decoration

Prepare chocolate egg according to step-by-step illustrations.

Place icing in pastry bag with medium writing tube affixed, then pipe trellis as shown. Let icing dry. Prepare chocolate leaves; make them very small. Place small amount melted chocolate on back of each leaf to hold firmly when pressed on seam of chocolate egg. Any shallow mold can be used for this process.

1. Be sure egg molds are thoroughly dry. Coat each mold generously with vegetable spray about 3 times.

2. Begin spreading melted chocolate at top of mold.

3. Work slowly, spreading chocolate evenly to at least ¼ inch thick.

4. Clean off edges if necessary; refrigerate several hours or overnight.

5. Loosen chocolate carefully with tip of sharp knife; tap mold gently on table.

6. Lift carefully or invert mold to remove chocolate egg.

7. Smooth rough edges from egg with very sharp knife; spread edge of one half with softened chocolate.

8. Press two halves together to join edges evenly.

9. Hold egg together just until edges are sealed.

how to melt chocolate chips

1. Pour package of chocolate chips into ovenproof bowl or pan. Place in warm oven at about 150°F.

2. Leave oven door slightly open. When chocolate chips have melted sufficiently, take out of oven. Softened, they will still have their original shape. Vigorously beat until they look like those above.

chocolate leaves

1. Wash rose leaves. Melt chocolate chips as instructed (see Index). Pull single leaf, upside down, over surface of melted chocolate.

2. Remove extra chocolate by tapping leaf against side of bowl. Place leaf chocolate-side-up on cookie sheet; put in refrigerator to harden.

3. When chocolate has chilled and hardened, peel off leaves. You'll have perfect chocolate leaves, with veins from real leaf imprinted in chocolate.

completed chocolate easter egg

candied violets

In France candied violets are used for cake decorations or to enhance a frozen soufflé or a dish of candy. Although they lend a cosmopolitan touch to gourmet desserts, they are very costly to buy in this country; but, if you have a little patience, you can make your own. Make them in spring when violets grow wild; store enough to use through the entire year.

Yield: 36

> **36 violets**
> **1 egg white**
> **½ cup sugar**
> **8 to 10 drops violet extract (optional)**
> **Purple food coloring (optional)**

Buy or pick 3 dozen violets. If picking them from your garden, be sure they have not been sprayed with pesticide. Remove stems, leaving just flower. Dry flowers very carefully with soft paper towel or tissue.

Beat egg white until foamy but not stiff. Dip each flower in egg white, then in sugar, coating thoroughly. Use toothpick to manipulate flowers, keeping petals open. Place flowers on cookie tin. Turn on oven to lowest heat for 5 minutes. Turn heat off; place pan of violets in oven. Let dry overnight. Will keep forever stored in airtight container in cool place.

If you wish to color violets a deeper purple than they are naturally, add a few drops of vegetable coloring to egg white before beating. If you want a violet flavor, add extract to egg white before beating. Violet extract is available in some drugstores and some gourmet food stores. It is not necessary if you cannot find it.

variations

Mint leaves or *rose petals* can be crystallized same as violets. It is not necessary to use added coloring or flavor for these leaves.

fondant dipping

A very creamy, sweet coating that can be flavored and tinted in any of your favorite colors and flavors can be developed from fondant. Make Basic Cooked Fondant (see Index); divide it into two portions. Cover tightly; store in the refrigerator at least 2 days before using. One portion can be used to form centers for dipping; vary the flavoring to suit your taste. The second portion will be used for coating.

Place portion of fondant you have reserved for coating in top of double boiler. Fill bottom with enough water so bottom of top pan does not touch water. Heat fondant over simmering, not boiling, water, stirring continually, until fondant is completely melted. Add any coloring or flavoring you prefer; remember, in adding color, pale pastels are prettier and more appetizing than strong colors. Heat fondant until quite hot and rather thin. Remove double boiler from heat; leave top pan with melted fondant over bottom pan so it will stay quite hot. As you work, a crust may form on top of fondant. If it does, just stir to remelt the crust. Since mixture is rather hot, you will not be able to work with your fingers. You will have to use a dipping fork to lift dipped candies. You can buy one from a commercial supplier or from a specialty kitchenware shop. Drop centers, one at a time, into hot fondant. Using dipping fork, pick up center with loop; allow excess fondant to drip back into pan. You will probably have to draw bottom of loop across edge of pan to wipe off excess from bottom of candy. Turn loop over; place warm candy on sheet of waxed paper. Allow to harden completely before moving. If you want, decorate still-warm candies with bits of chopped nuts, silver shot, candy sprinkles, or tiny rosettes of Icing (see Index).

Fondants do not keep as well as other chocolates. After about a week they begin to harden and crack, so make only as many as you plan to use within one week.

If you have leftover fondant coating, you can make party mints—or other flavors—by dropping melted fondant from teaspoon onto level, lightly oiled cookie tin. They will form round patties that can be served as is or dipped in chocolate. Use same amount of fondant each time, so patties will be uniform in size. These will keep better than dipped candies, because it doesn't matter if they become crisp in texture. Store all fondants in airtight container in cool but not cold place.

summer coating

A popular candy coating that is very easy to use is a white coating sometimes called *summer chocolate.* As a matter of fact, it is not chocolate at all and is low in cholesterol, so it is especially popular with those who are trying to control their cholesterol intake and still have a sweet treat once in a while. It is easy to use because it has a much higher melting point than chocolate, so you don't have to worry about the weather when you use it, and it does not streak like chocolate does. You can buy it in bulk from a commercial supplier—do not use already-prepared candy or candy bars made from this coating; other ingredients will have been added and it won't coat the centers properly.

Grate 1 pound summer coating; melt in top of double boiler over simmering but not boiling water. Do not let bottom of top pan touch water. Do not allow water to come to boil. Stir coating with wide wooden spoon or rubber spatula until completely melted. Remove top pan from hot water. Stir coating; let cool to 100°F—just above body temperature. When cooled to this point, you can add food coloring and flavoring; be very careful not to let any moisture get into coating. A slab is not necessary for dipping—you can use dipping fork or your fingers and dip directly in pan of melted coating, using same method described in Chocolate Dipping (see Index). If mixture cools too much, place it over hot water to remelt, stirring very well so temperature is uniform.

If you have any leftover summer coating, use it by mixing with nuts, coconut, or chopped dried fruit and dropping from teaspoon onto waxed paper. Be sure to toast nuts and coconut first to produce a really tasty, professional-type candy.

Any centers suitable for dipping in chocolate are also very good dipped in summer coating.

Hint: If you are going to color coating, start with just a drop or two of food coloring. You can always make it a little darker if necessary, but it is the very pale pastel tints that make appetizing candy.

3 varieties of bark, nuts, and cherries used in semisweet-chocolate and summer coating

caramel coating

It is possible to coat some centers with caramels—those that can withstand fairly high heat without melting. Marshmallows, jellies, soft fondant, and divinity are all unsuitable for caramel dipping because they will start to melt and become sticky as soon as they are dipped into hot caramel coating. Also, you will have to roll the freshly dipped centers into something else, such as ground or chopped nuts, coconut, or candy sprinkles, because caramel coating by itself is just too sticky to handle nicely.

Make 1 recipe Caramels (see Index). Let syrup cool to about 145°F before dipping. If syrup cools down too much while you are still dipping, place it on barely warm heat to thin out enough to work with. If you have a coffee warmer, this is a very convenient heater to place pan on. You will have to use a dipping fork; syrup will be too hot for fingers. Follow directions for Fondant Dipping (see Index), but roll each dipped candy in dry coating of your choice. Chopped nuts make an especially good final coating for caramels. Use any leftover caramel syrup to make Turtles (see Index).

candy centers coated with caramel and rolled in nuts

icing

Cake icings are a very special category of candy. While we rarely think of them as candy, that is exactly what they are. Of course, there is an endless variety of icings and special ways to use them but, since volumes have been written on this subject alone, I will include only one basic recipe—an icing that is used not only on cakes, but for decorating candy. It can be tinted any color you choose and with an icing bag and a variety of tips you will be able to write names, make rosettes, and make any other appropriate designs.

basic decorating icing

7 cups confectioners' sugar, sifted
Juice of 1 lemon
3 egg whites, unbeaten

Combine sugar, lemon juice, and 1 egg white in large mixing bowl. Stir with wooden spoon until mixture is of spreading consistency. Add rest of egg whites as needed. Icing should be stiff enough to hold its shape but pliable enough to go through icing tube easily. You can use food coloring to tint any or all of the icing, as you wish.

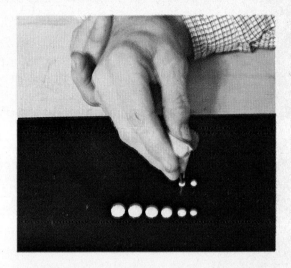

1. To get feel of using icing bag, play around a little each time you begin. Here we show how to lay down lines, using plain writing tube. Note tube is not placed on surface but is held a fraction above it. This is very important in controlling the line. Squeeze with even, steady pressure to make line consistent in size.

2. It is easy to achieve a professional touch with artistic rosettes. They are very effective, yet simple to make. Using medium star tube, make varying sizes by using different amounts of pressure on icing bag. Pressure of hand gripping icing bag determines size of each rosette. Allow icing mixture to touch decorating surface, push in gently, then pull bag back quickly, leaving rosette on candy.

3. Starting with set of lines you have practiced, form trellis by crossing lines. Note that hands are clear of working surface. Do not drag tube through other lines.

4. Here we see completed design. If you like, you can now put tiny "dots" at each intersection of lines for an even more decorative look.

sugarless candy

There are many people who, for one reason or another, cannot eat sugar. With them in mind I have included these recipes that do not use any sugar except that contained in the fruit itself. Raisins, figs, dates, orange juice, and grape juice are all very sweet naturally and can be used to make delicious confections. Unsweetened grated or shredded coconut can be found in almost any health-food store and is particularly good in this type of confection, because the natural flavor, without any added sweetening, is distinctive and delicious. I prefer using white, unsweetened grape juice rather than the more common purple, since it has the same good flavor but adds no color to the finished confection. It can be found in many supermarkets and almost all specialty shops.

It is much easier to make unsweetened confections in a food processor than in a blender, since the mixtures tend to be very sticky and it is easier to empty the container of a food processor. However, whichever you use, be very careful not to overblend or overmix the fruit and nuts. Allow the ingredients to retain some character and texture rather than becoming just a mushy mix.

raisins

almonds

assorted nuts with "mamma's special"

mamma's special

By any name, it's delicious! In our house it's just called Mamma's Special because there is always a bowl to dip into, and everyone, young and old, likes it.

Yield: 1-quart mix

1 cup unsalted peanuts
1 cup walnut meats
1 cup raisins
¼ cup toasted sunflower seeds

¼ cup pumpkin seeds
½ cup small sesame crackers
Handful of unsweetened
   coconut chips

Toss all ingredients together in large bowl. Place serving spoon in bowl and watch mix disappear.

date special

Add ½ cup pitted dates, cut in half, to above mixture.

sweet special

This is *not* sugarless! To above mix add ½ cup chopped, candied pineapple and ½ cup banana chips.

coconut delights

Yield: 24 ¾-inch balls

1 cup raisins
1 cup walnut meats
½ teaspoon cinnamon
½ teaspoon grated orange rind
1 tablespoon undiluted frozen orange
**   concentrate**
¾ cup grated or shredded
**   unsweetened coconut**

Chop raisins and walnuts coarsely. Mix with cinnamon, orange rind and juice, and ¼ cup coconut. Form into ¾-inch balls; roll in remaining coconut. Let dry an hour before serving. Will keep well about a week in refrigerator.

Try using white raisins instead of the usual variety, and substitute grape juice for orange juice.

date delights

Use above mixture to stuff pitted dates. Some stuffed dates can then be rolled in coconut and some left plain, to make an interesting contrast when served.

sherry balls

Substitute 1 tablespoon dry sherry for orange juice in above recipe.

peanut butter

Peanut butter is a very tasty and extremely useful binder for fruit and nuts in sugarless confections. Some commercial peanut butter contains sugar, so if you want to be sure it is totally pure and sugarless, make it at home. This is very, very easy.

Purchase unsalted, blanched peanuts—again, your convenient health-food store is the source. Using steel blade of food processor, add nuts to container; process them until you have a creamy, easy to spread peanut butter. The longer nuts are processed, the creamier the spread becomes. You do not want to reduce them to oil, so do not overprocess. You will be able to tell very easily when the proper consistency is reached.

peanutties

Yield: 24 ½-inch balls

   1 cup very coarsely chopped peanuts
   1 cup very coarsely chopped raisins
   ½ cup peanut butter
   ¼ cup very finely chopped or ground
      peanuts

Blend together coarsely chopped peanuts, raisins, and peanut butter. Form into small balls; roll in ground peanuts. Dry 1 or 2 hours before serving.

Use mixture to stuff dates or prunes. Since this is not sweet, it makes an extremely good after-school snack—full of energy-making food, but not appetite spoiling.

Unsalted cashew nuts can be substituted for peanuts in above recipe. Cashew butter is made exactly the same way as peanut butter. Most stores sell broken cashew nuts at considerably less cost than whole beauties. By all means buy these for use in the butter, or for that matter, in any candy where you do not need whole, perfect nuts.

fruit and nut bars

Yield: 32 1 × 2-inch bars

   2 cups walnuts
   1 cup raisins
   1 cup dates
   ¼ teaspoon cinnamon
   ¼ teaspoon grated orange rind
   4 tablespoons Grape Jel

Coarsely chop walnuts, raisins, and dates. Blend with other ingredients. Spread in oiled 8 × 8 × 2-inch pan. Chill thoroughly. Slice into 1 × 2-inch bars with very sharp knife. Refrigerate until served. Will keep several days in refrigerator.

Fruits and nuts can be varied in this recipe. Please your taste, but remember to keep the quantity at a total of 4 cups of fruit and nuts. Be sure nuts are unsalted.

grape jel

   ½ cup grape juice
   1 teaspoon unflavored gelatin

Boil grape juice in small saucepan until reduced to ½ its volume or ¼ cup. Add gelatin to hot liquid; stir until completely dissolved. Use in above recipe while still warm; it will become very stiff when cold.

date and nut balls

Yield: 24 ¾-inch balls

    1 cup pitted dates
    1 cup walnut meats
    ¼ teaspoon grated orange rind
    1 tablespoon undiluted frozen orange
        concentrate
    ¼ cup finely chopped walnuts

Using steel blade of food processor or blender, chop dates into fairly large chunks. Add walnuts; blend together until well mixed, but do not allow mixture to become a paste. Add orange rind and juice. Form into ¾-inch balls; roll in finely chopped nuts. Allow to dry an hour or two before serving. These keep well about a week in the refrigerator. Leftover chopped nuts can be saved and used in another recipe.

Grape juice can be substituted for orange juice for a subtle flavor change.

cinnamon balls

Add ¼ teaspoon cinnamon to above mixture.

fig and nut balls

Substitute 1 cup figs for dates in above recipe. If you use moist figs, you may want to add a little less juice; dried figs may require a few drops more.

packaging

You have turned out a batch of creamy fudge. You have mastered brittles and caramels. The chocolates you have dipped are delicious and beautiful. You want to give some to friends. Okay. How do you package?

I am proud of the confections that come out of my kitchen, and I want everyone to know that I made them. I have colorful labels that I bought in a stationery store. They start out saying: "From the kitchen of . . . ." There is space for the date and description of the contents. You fill in the appropriate information. I use these labels on all gifts of food.

I save bags, boxes, and some cans. Lined with fancy doilies and waxed paper, covered with gift paper, I can turn a plain container into a festive package—and you can, too.

For the simplest package, I use a small, plain paper bag, measuring 4½ × 8 inches. One large-size plastic sandwich bag fits nicely inside and after it is filled with the candy of your choice the top can be secured with a twistee, and it is airtight. Paste a label on the front of the bag. Fold over the top; staple to secure. For a more festive effect, buy colorful bags. Fill them, and secure the tops with ribbons tied with fancy bows.

Cover the lid of a plain box with fancy paper. To do this, measure the width of the box and add the measurements of the sides. Measure the length of the lid in the same way. Do not forget to include the sides. Cut a piece of paper a little larger than the box lid plus the sides. Place the box lid upside down on the wrong side of the paper, centering the lid. Fold the paper carefully into the inside of the lid, one side at a time, mitering the corners. Secure the paper with transparent sticky tape. Turn the lid over and admire! Line the bottom of the box with fancy paper doilies, allowing the edges of the doilies to be an inch or two higher than the top of the box. Place a piece of waxed paper on the bottom of the box; arrange the candies you have selected on the paper. Try to fill the box completely, so the candy won't move around. If you are going to give a lot of candy gifts, you might want to buy a supply of the small, fluted candy cases that professionals use. These can be obtained from a commercial supply house. After the box is filled, fold the edges of the doilies down over the candy. Place the covered box top on. Finish with your personal label. Decorate with ribbons and bows if you want.

One-pound coffee tins make good containers for brittles, marshmallows, divinity, or any bulky candies. Choose a pretty paper. Measure the can around the middle. Measure the length of the side. Cut a piece of paper long enough to wrap around the can with a little overlap, but try to cut the exact length of the side. Wrap the paper around and secure with double-face sticky tape cut to the exact length and placed along the edge of the paper. Wrap the paper around the can carefully; allow the overlap to cover the edge of the paper where you have placed the double-face sticky tape. The double-face sticky tape will then secure both edges. Use colored tape around the bottom and top edges to finish. Or, if you have been very careful and cut exactly, put a piece of double-face sticky tape along the top edge of the can and one along the bottom edge and very carefully tape the paper to the can in this way. Save the plastic lid that comes with the can to use, as is, for a sealed top. Again, finish off with your personal label. For added decor, place a fancy paper doily of the proper size under the plastic lid, allowing the edges to show around the lid.

I buy strawberries in pint-size plastic baskets. These baskets, lined with paper doilies, make marvelous containers for any of your homemade confections. Allow some of the doily to show around the top; fasten a large bow on one side for extra color. Wrap the entire basket in plastic wrap.

Children love to decorate cans and boxes with cutouts and pictures; by all means let them help you in packaging your sweets. Let your imagination run wild. Look around your kitchen for unique items to use. You will be surprised at what you find.

Note: For handling dipped chocolates you might want to use a clean pair of white work gloves so you won't smudge the candy with fingerprints.

If you are going to send candy through the mail, be sure to select candy that will withstand some rough treatment and change of temperature. Most fudge, caramels, marshmallows, jellies, brittles, and firm-centered chocolates can be mailed, if packaged properly. I pack the candy in a fancy box first. I place that box in a larger, heavy-duty mailing box, filling the space all around with dry, unsalted, unbuttered popcorn! This cushions the candy and is edible at the end of the journey!

I hope you have fun making, eating, and sharing the candy in this book and that the suggestions here have helped to spark your imagination so that you go on to make a wide variety of satisfying sweets.

candy assortment and gift wrappings

index

128